HAPPY BIRTHDAY
2001

Love Mom

The
Good Health
Adventure
Cook Book

The Good Health Adventure Cook Book

EXCITING VEGETARIAN AND SEAFOOD RECIPES FOR BUSY PEOPLE

BY
ROWAN
BISHOP

David Bateman

First published as *The Good Health Adventure Cook Book*

This new edition first published in 1998 by David Bateman Ltd,
30 Tarndale Grove, Albany, Auckland, New Zealand

ISBN 1 86953 388 7

Illustrations by Caroline Campbell

Cover design by Sue Reidy

Printed by Colorcraft

Preface

Over the 12 years I have been experimenting with food, I
have been developing ideas within the new cuisine which is
based upon increasing concern about health and the demand
for a more cosmopolitan and adventurous approach to taste.
These new directions are drawn from aspects of flavouring
and methods from cuisines around the world, and use this
variety specifically to address health concerns. There has
been a shift to a much more balanced diet in terms of
reducing the amount of saturated fat consumed, a greater
emphasis on unrefined carbohydrate and an increased
consumption of fibre, fresh fruits and fresh vegetables.
It is well recognised that, while red meat in itself is not
harmful, traditionally we have eaten too much meat as the
focal point of meals and relied upon it for protein, neglecting
the fact that protein is contained in plant foods as well, in
conjunction with much greater amounts of fibre and fewer
saturated fats than are found in meat.
Seafood is relatively light and easy to digest; it is also our
major source of omega 3's, a group of unsaturated fatty
acids known to modify the events in heart disease so that
heart attacks are less likely. They make the blood less likely
to clot, and may help to reduce blood pressure. Fish contains
few saturated fats and has very low levels of cholesterol.
Nearly all fish has fewer calories than meats with nearly as
much protein — mussels actually contain more iron than red
meats.
This book is not intended as a stringent nutritional text for
those who have medically diagnosed conditions. It is a
generalised, prevention-is-better-than-cure compilation of
recipes drawn from cuisines around the world, which
concentrates on providing plenty of interest and taste appeal
while embracing current health concerns. Many of the
recipes are balanced one-dish meals for four to six, the
emphasis being on busy people who have little time to spare
but need to eat healthily — and those who love food.

Acknowledgements

ginger root

This book is dedicated to my husband Russell. Without his help, support and encouragement this book would never have progressed beyond being a pile of notes in a corner somewhere. Also to our children, Matthew, James, Stephanie and Sam, for their tolerance as I trialled dishes over a year, day after day and often four times in a row. Warmest and grateful thanks to Sue Carruthers, my friend and partner in *The Vegetarian Adventure Cook Book*, for her support and contribution of several recipes and ideas to this book.

Also to many friends around Paremata and Wellington who lent their support, offered their ideas and proved their willingness to do a final trial and comment on recipes: Peter Saggers (quality control and willing taster) and Jacqui; Bronwyn Anderson (chief of trialling and encouragement) and daughter Debbie; also Jan Cox; Jean Dickenson and Rod Young; Julie Simenson; Sheryl Perera; Cushla Bretton; Jo Hine; Robin McLennan; Rex Bloomfield and Tricia Thompson; Bev Metsers; Bev Mateparae; Susie Nichols; Lynne Cartwright; Adrienne Jansen; Judy McCoy; Wanda Peck, whose help extended far beyond the call of duty; Jean Phipps and the New Zealand Fishing Industry Board, and Dr Mike Lyons, for their support, and willingness to provide access to information and resource material; and many more whose encouragement helped enormously.

Contents

SEAFOOD

RECIPES TO KEEP AT YOUR RIGHT HAND

DESSERTS AND FILLINGS FOR THOSE GAPS

Sponsors

It is difficult to know how to thank these sponsors adequately for their courtesy and their generosity in supplying fresh products for trialling throughout the work on this book. It would not have been possible to include the number or range of fish and seafood recipes without wholehearted and unquestioning support from Talleys, Skeggs and Kiwiclams. My grateful thanks to them and also to Mainland Products for a supply of cheeses for recipe development.

Talleys Seafoods Ltd
P O Box 5
Motueka

Skeggs Foods Ltd
8 Lorne St
Wellington

Kiwiclams
P O Box 378
Nelson

Mainland Products Ltd
70 Macandrew Road
Dunedin

Some Food Facts

The following is not intended to be the whole story on nutritional facts, but rather just a few salient points of interest pertinent to current health concerns and, in particular, to this book.

Variety, Balance and Common Sense

No one food supplies all the essential nutrients you need; variety is essential to ensure a well-balanced diet. Apart from meat, there are four main food groups to choose from which will ensure a well-balanced diet with all the vitamins, minerals and nutrients necessary to ensure good health. Whether or not you include some meat in your diet is entirely a matter of choice. In this book seafood is included as an adjunct to these four main groups (see preface).

1. Grains, legumes (including pulses), nuts and seeds.
2. Fresh vegetables.
3. Fresh fruit.
4. Dairy products and eggs.

Grains, legumes, nuts and seeds are the major sources of protein in the plant world; it is perfectly possible to have an adequate protein complement in your diet from these sources, plus groups 2 and 3, although this kind of diet (vegan) necessitates some knowledge of basic nutritional principles. The inclusion of dairy products and eggs greatly decreases the chances of any deficiency.

Most vegetarians include milk, cheese and eggs in their diet; these foods are major sources of protein, calcium and Vitamin B12 as well as many other nutrients, and vastly increase the scope of tastes and textures available. They also greatly increase the number of dishes accessible to small children and their specific digestion needs.

Proteins

Proteins are essential to life and the maintenance of the cells and tissues of the body, but they cannot be manufactured or stored by the body. They are made up of smaller units called amino acids, of which there are about 20, eight of which must be supplied in the food we eat. These eight essential amino acids must also be supplied at the same meal and in the right proportion. Now don't panic, just read on . . .

Animal and fish protein foods contain all the amino acids in correct proportions, whereas plant protein foods generally lack one or more of the essential amino acids. By an intake of certain combinations of plant foods, however, you can supply your body with protein which is just as good as that in animal proteins. The word 'combinations' sometimes causes a good deal of anxiety, but there really is no

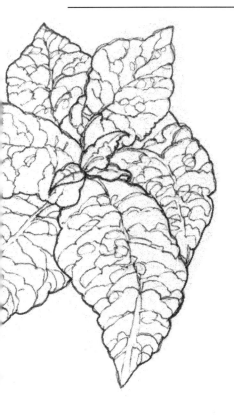

foundation for this. The key, again, is variety — and simple principles kept in mind to ensure balance.

For example, all legumes/pulses, together with grains, produce a complete, high quality protein, and all cultures have staple dishes combining these two — such as baked beans on toast, dhal and chapati or rice; even a peanut butter sandwich provides an excellent combination of amino acids (bread as a grain product and peanut butter as a legume product).

By happy coincidence, these combinations taste good together as well as being nutritionally complementary. Nuts and seeds add variety to an enormous range of dishes, as well as providing a complete protein when used in conjunction with legumes/pulses. Take hummus, for example, the popular Middle Eastern dip made from a chickpea base and tahini (sesame seed paste).

There are, of course, many different combinations which produce complete protein, some of them classic ones such as macaroni cheese, and it requires only a little thought and common sense for such planning to become second nature. Protein concern in our diets has been overemphasised; if your energy needs are being met with a reasonable variety of whole foods, you should be getting all the protein you need.

Fibre

Fibre is a constituent of all plants, and there are two types.
1. Cellulosic or insoluble fibre
This is made up largely of the walls of plants. This type of fibre absorbs water and is important for the proper functioning of the gastro-intestinal tract, including the bowels. It is significant to note that bowel cancer is virtually unknown among vegetarians. Refined products such as white rice and flour have been stripped of this fibre (as well as many of the vitamins and nutrients otherwise available). Whereas it was previously thought that a large proportion of fibre in plants remained indigestible, it is now known that all fibre is at least partially digested. This digestion takes place because of the action of bacteria in the digestive tract — fermentation. A breakdown product of this is butyric acid, a substance known to reduce the possibility of cancer-forming cells, especially in the bowel.
2. Soluble fibre
This type of fibre has been the subject of increased scrutiny in recent times, especially with the heightened concern over cholesterol levels. This type of fibre includes mucilage, gums and pectin and is known to help in the stabilising of blood sugar levels, and in lowering the amount of fats and cholesterol in the blood.

Fruits such as apples, blackberries, pears, strawberries and plums contain significant quantities of soluble fibre, along with vegetables such as all the legumes (e.g. peas, beans) and pulses, broccoli, zucchini, carrots and tomatoes and okra. Oatbran has a particularly high concentration, but soluble fibre is also contained in smaller amounts in ordinary rolled oats, rye, barley, sesame seeds and brown rice.

A high fibre diet is useful in weight control as it is low in calories but high in bulk — in other words, the eater feels satisfied without consuming large amounts of calories. It's very difficult to gain or maintain excess weight if your diet is high in unrefined foods.

Because it takes several hours for foods high in fibre to be digested, you have a valuable spread of energy over time and you don't feel the need for constant 'topping up' between meals. This is also important for diabetics since they must avoid a sudden increase in blood sugar levels after meals. Water soluble fibre contains a gel which slows down the rate at which food is emptied from the stomach to the small intestine, so that blood sugar levels are 'smoothed out' and stabilised.

Please note that the usefulness of pectic substances is affected by their preparation. This is why it's better to steam vegetables and leave fruits and vegetables unpeeled as much as possible.

Cholesterol and Fats

Cholesterol is virtually unknown in the plant world, being found almost exclusively in animal products such as meats, dairy products and egg yolks. It should be noted that cholesterol is important to health in that it is a major part of cell membranes , digestive juices (bile) and sexual hormones. Our livers manufacture 80% of the cholesterol contained in our bodies; the other 20% we take in in the food we eat.

Excess cholesterol is the problem: it can be deposited in the arteries and cause blockages which can lead to heart attacks. The consumption of too much saturated fat actually causes the body to produce more cholesterol. Thus the amount of saturated fats we eat is regarded as a more crucial causal factor leading to heart disease than the amount of dietary cholesterol.

Cholesterol is converted into bile acids in the liver, and the body normally reabsorbs more than 90% of these (used in the digestive process). Water soluble fibre, however, binds the bile acids in the large intestine and they are excreted in the faeces. To make up the loss, the liver draws cholesterol from the blood, therefore reducing the blood cholesterol level.

'Good' and 'Bad' Cholesterol Carriers

Two main vehicles are responsible for carrying cholesterol around the body. These are HDL (high density lipoprotein) and LDL (low density lipoprotein).

LDL carries cholesterol through the bloodstream and into

the arteries, where any excess may be deposited. HDL cleans out excess cholesterol and carries it out of the bloodstream and into the liver. So HDL is good, whereas LDL can do a lot of damage. The balance between these two is important, and it is here and in the functioning of the liver that genetic factors can play a part in cholesterol levels and heart disease, along with other factors such as smoking, high blood pressure, diabetes, lack of exercise, excess weight and stress. Although between 60% and 70% of New Zealanders are estimated to have cholesterol levels which are too high, the whole picture of risk factors need to be looked at with any one individual. Also, there is a margin of error factor in testing for cholesterol, to the extent that it can vary up to about 0.5% between one test and another. It does, however, give a valuable indication of levels.

All in all, then, there is significant evidence to suggest that we should reduce our intake of saturated fats and increase our intake of fibre, both soluble and insoluble.

Fats and Oils

Mention has already been made of the harmful effects of a diet too high in saturated fats and its association with blood cholesterol levels. Avoid them as much as possible in favour of polyunsaturated or, even better, monounsaturated fats, keeping in mind, of course, that all fats are essentially fats, and too much of any kind is not in the best interests of good health.

Emphasis has recently gone from the cholesterol-lowering polyunsaturated fats (e.g. safflower oil) to the monounsaturated (e.g. olive oil, also found in avocados and peanut butter). These fats lower LDL but leave HDL alone.

So, if you eat a variety of foods, especially whole and fresh foods, and combine this with some good old-fashioned common sense and moderation you will achieve a balanced, nutritious and healthy diet suited to your particular needs. With the exception of some highly refined foods, few foods are of little or no use to us. The danger lies with the consumption of any food or food group to excess and/or to the exclusion of others.

Kitchen Aids

Food Processor
I regard a food processor as an essential kitchen tool, and have geared my recipes accordingly. A blender, however, will suffice in many instances.

Microwave
Highly recommended, a microwave is a wonderful time saver for the busy cook. A basic model is fine, since you rarely need a very sophisticated one. I have not given specific instructions for microwaving, as the types and voltages differ so much. Get a good book, and learn how to use your own model; then you can adapt recipes to suit. Cooking times where given are approximate only, but based on a 600w model.
I tend to use a microwave for steps in the cooking process; this approach can be expanded according to individual preference. For example, I prefer not to microwave pastry or breads, but of course it is possible.

Wok
A wok is wonderful for stir fries, etc.

Pressure Cooker
This harmless but efficient aid is a marvellous help in the kitchen, especially if you don't have a microwave. (Cooking dried beans is simple with one of these.)

Steamer
You'll find a steamer very useful, mostly for vegetables.

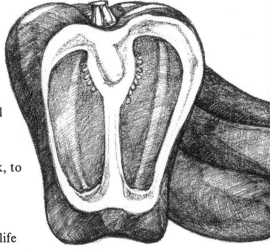

Omelette/Crepe Pan
Keep this for one use only!

Measuring Spoons and Cups
These are essential. This book is geared to the use of level metric measures to ensure the most reliable results.

Knives
A range of sharp knives is necessary for any kitchen work, to facilitate and speed up preparation.

Wooden Spoons, Whisk, Set of Bowls and Saucepans
All these pieces of kitchen equipment are vital and make life much less complicated.

Electric Beater
This is necessary, although a small hand-held beater is quite adequate.

The Pantry Shelf

A well-stocked pantry can make meal preparation a real joy instead of a chore. There is nothing quite so frustrating as deciding on a recipe only to find that one or more of the essential ingredients is missing. The following is a guide for stocking your shelves, especially for those who are new to vegetarian cooking. It's a good idea to collect glass jars with tight-fitting lids. Dried pasta, beans, dried fruit, grains and seeds make an attractive display stored in jars, and this storage method saves hunting around in the back of a dark cupboard.

chickpeas

peanuts

Dried Beans

Aduki beans, black beans, broad beans, chickpeas, kidney beans, lentils, lima beans, mung beans, pinto and soya beans, split and whole peas.

Storage: Display in lidded glass jars. Store any excess in labelled clear bags in the freezer.

To cook beans: Beans should be washed well, then soaked overnight or for several hours. Use 3 times as much water as beans and cook until tender, depending on the type of bean.
A pressure cooker is a great time-saver. Pre-soaking is not necessary. Wash and place in pressure cooker with 3-4 times as much water.

	Soak/Boil	Pressure Cook
Chickpeas	2½ hours	45–50 minutes
Pinto beans	1½ hours	30 minutes
Lima beans	1 hour	25 minutes
Kidney beans	1¼ hours	25 minutes
Split peas	30 minutes	10-12 minutes
Soya beans	3 hours	50-55 minutes

Refresh immediately under cold running water and drain. Beans can also be cooked, covered, in a microwave.

Seeds

Alfalfa seeds, pumpkin kernels, caraway seeds, poppy seeds, sunflower kernels, sesame seeds.

Storage: Store in glass jars for a limited time, as seeds do go rancid. It's best to store the bulk in the freezer in well-labelled bags. Sprouted beans and seeds keep well in the refrigerator for up to a week.

Dried Fruit

Apples, apricots, currants, raisins, desiccated coconut, dates, figs, peaches, pears, sultanas.
Candied peel, crystallised ginger and cherries.

Storage: Display in a cool place in glass jars for up to 6 months. Store any excess in the freezer.

Grains and Flours

White flour
Self-raising flour
Storage: Keep in a container or jar for up to 6 months. Freeze any excess. Limited shelf life.

Wholemeal flour
Storage: Limited shelf life. Freeze excess in sealed containers or bags.

Arrowroot, cornmeal, cornflour, chickpea flour, soy flour
Storage: Good storage life if kept in well-sealed containers.
Wheatgerm, bran, rolled oats, bulghar or kibbled wheat, breakfast cereals, barley, etc. Storage as wholemeal flour.

Rice

White and brown. Brown rice cooks very quickly in a pressure cooker. Place in the cooker with twice the volume of water and cook for 15 minutes.

Storage: White rice keeps well.
Keep a well-sealed jar of brown rice on display and freeze any excess to keep it from turning mildewed or rancid.

Nuts

Almonds, brazils, cashews, hazelnuts, macadamias, peanuts, pecans, pine nut kernels, walnuts.

Storage: Limited shelf life. Keep in well-sealed containers up to 3 months. Store excess in freezer. Check nuts carefully when purchasing, as they do tend to go rancid easily.

Dried Pasta

Cannelloni, lasagne, macaroni, noodles, spaghetti, rigatoni, tagliatelli, etc.

Storage: Excellent shelf life if kept well sealed.

Wholemeal pasta and buckwheat pasta
Storage: Limited shelf life. Store excess in freezer.

Stored Goods

Although it's of course more desirable to use fresh vegetables, it's still convenient and practical to have a good range of tinned goods in the store cupboard, and frozen vegetables and fruits in the freezer.
Tinned vegetables have a shelf life of up to 2 years; tinned fruits have a shelf life of up to 3 years. Frozen fruit and vegetables may be kept for up to 1 year.

Tinned Foods

Artichokes, asparagus, bamboo shoots, beans and pulses such as soy beans, chickpeas, kidney beans, etc., beetroot, baby carrots, corn, green beans, mushrooms, tomatoes — whole peeled, puree and paste, savoury and tomato juice.
Vegetarian soups — handy for quick casserole and pasta dishes.
Vegetarian tinned nutmeats — good for rissoles and savoury bakes.
Vegetarian soya bean protein products — there are a variety on the market. I personally do not like the meat substitutes, such as burgers and sausages, so these products are not used in this book.

Fruit

Apples, apricots, blueberries, blackberries, blackcurrants, boysenberries, cherries, kiwifruit, gooseberries, guavas, lychees, mangoes, mandarins, passionfruit, pears, peaches, raspberries, strawberries.

shell pasta

Herbs and Spices

It's a good idea to grow your own herbs, even if you only have a tiny balcony and no garden. Herbs will grow in a sunny, sheltered position in small pots, and young plants are available from most nurseries. Dried herbs, however, still have an essential place in the kitchen. (Try microwaving your own.)

Herbs

Bay leaves, chives, dill, fennel, lemon grass, mint, marjoram, oregano, parsley, rosemary, sage, sweet basil, tarragon, thyme.

Storage: Keep in small jars away from heat and light. Shelf life is 2 months only, otherwise herbs can go musty. Keep any excess in the freezer.

Spices

Allspice, caraway, cardamom, anise, cayenne or chilli, celery seeds, cinnamon, cumin, fenugreek, five spice, ginger, mustard seeds, nutmeg, paprika, peppercorns, poppy seeds, saffron, turmeric.

Storage: Spices also go musty and lose their flavour after several months. Use up quickly and store any excess in the freezer.

Tamarind is available in a dried, pressed form from oriental stores and some supermarkets. Soak in boiling water 15 minutes and then press liquid through a strainer. Good in curries.

Curry Powder

A good quality curry powder is important.

Condiments and Sauces

Salt, Mustard

There are now herb 'salts' plus several other alternatives available for those who wish to cut down on their salt intake.
A good variety of wholegrain mustards are now available.

Sauces

Apple, black bean, chilli or tabasco, soya, mint, horseradish, mayonnaise, tomato or ketchup, Worcester, fish sauce (nam pla), hoi sin, oyster.

Peanut Butter

Peanut butter is of use in baking and also in oriental sauces and salad dressings.

Stock

It's a simple matter to make your own stock. Collect well-washed vegetable peelings except for onion skins and cabbage. Barely cover with water and simmer gently, covered, for 1 hour. Cool and strain. Freeze in covered containers.

Preserves

Jams and jellies, chutneys, capers, pickles and relishes, green peppercorns, green and black olives.

Oils and Vinegars

Corn oil, soya bean oil, sunflower oil, nut oils and seed oils, olive oil.
There are a large variety of fruit, malt and herb vinegars available.
Buy the best quality oils. Nut and seed oils and olive are expensive, but well worth the investment. Make your own fruit and herb vinegars. Use plain wine vinegar and steep dried herbs or fruit in it for several weeks.

Other Flavouring Ingredients

Coconut cream (tinned), Marmite or yeast extract, instant soups and stocks, miso paste.

dill

Baking and Desserts

Baking powder, baking soda, tartaric acid, dried yeast, dried milk powder, evaporated milk, condensed milk, honey, custard powder, vanilla and almond essence.

Cocoa and Coffee

As these are high in caffeine, you may prefer to use carob powder and bars available from health food stores.

Gelatine

As gelatine is an animal product, you may prefer to use agar-agar, a seaweed product with excellent setting properties.

White sugar, brown sugar, caster sugar, icing sugar

Honey can be used instead of sugar if you wish.

Other Useful Items

There are now a number of 'long life' foods available which need no refrigeration until after opening. They include:

cream
milk
fruit juice
tofu (an excellent Japanese brand is now available)
These items have a shelf life of 6 months before opening. Note: Fresh tofu is readily available in most supermarkets and freezes very well.

Easy Measures for Common Ingredients

In compiling this book, I used level metric measures as our standard for all recipes.

Solids

	Cups	Imperial	Metric
Breadcrumbs (fresh)	1	2 oz	60 g
Butter or margarine	¼ cup	2 oz	60 g
Cheese (grated)	1½ cups	6 oz	180 g
Flour (sifted)	1 cup	4 oz	125 g
Lentils or beans (raw)	1½ cups	8 oz	250 g
Nuts (chopped)	¼ cup	1 oz	30 g
Macaroni (uncooked)	1½ cups	6 oz	180 g
Rice (uncooked)	1 cup	6 oz	180 g
(cooked)	1 cup	6 oz	180 g
Sugar	¼ cup	2 oz	60 g
	1 cup	8 oz	250 g

The actual exact conversion is 1 oz = 28.35g. For easy reference it is recommended to convert as follows:

1 oz = 30g	2 oz = 60g	4 oz = 125g
6 oz = 180g	8 oz = 250g	10 oz = 300g
12 oz = 360g	14 oz = 425g	16 oz = 480g
1 kg = 2.2 lb		

Liquid Measure

The exact conversions is 1 pint = 568 ml. For easy reference it is recommended to convert as follows:
½ cup = 125 ml
1 cup = 250 ml
1½ cups = 375 ml
2 cups = 500 ml
4 cups = 1 litre

Soups

Pumpkin and Kumara Curry Soup

There seems to be no end to learning about spices and herbs in the flavouring of food. The possible combinations, given just the major cuisines, is infinite, and the teasing and exhilarating thing is that no one person will ever know all there is to know. All we can do is to learn, listen, watch and taste. Sometimes flavouring should be minimal, if present at all; at others it should assert itself to a greater or lesser extent. But as long as you enjoy food, *never* be indifferent.

This soup is not hot — it contains no chillies — but it is flavoured with a very interesting blend of base curry spices combined with basil. It sounds quite unusual, but it works well, and the result is a most popular soup, quick, economical and a meal in itself if served in generous portions with wholemeal bread, a selection of cheeses and a salad/fresh fruit if you wish.

This soup may be microwaved. Freezes well.

750g prepared (peeled) pumpkin
550g prepared (peeled) kumara
6 cups stock or water
1 tsp turmeric
1 tbsp ground coriander
1 tbsp garam masala
2 tsp curry powder
2-2½ tsp salt
1 tbsp dried basil
plain yoghurt and chopped parsley or fresh coriander for garnish

Chop the pumpkin and kumara into large dice, about 3cm. Place in a large saucepan or pressure cooker with all the remaining ingredients.
If cooking in a saucepan, cover and bring to the boil, then reduce the heat and simmer for 25-30 minutes, stirring once or twice. If you are using a pressure cooker, cook for approximately 10 minutes at pressure.
There is no need to puree this soup before serving — mashing it thoroughly with a potato masher seems to be sufficient.
Serve accompanied by plain yoghurt if desired, and a sprinkle of chopped parsley or fresh coriander.

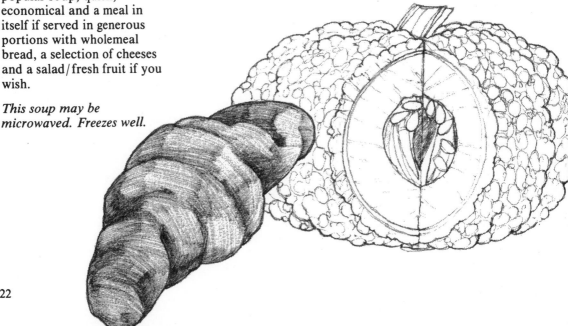

Spiced Parsnip and Mushroom Soup

1 kg parsnips
1 cup chopped mushrooms
6 cups water
¾ cup yellow split peas
1 tbsp ground cumin
2 tsp ground coriander
1 tsp five spice powder*
2-2½ tsp salt
lots of freshly ground black pepper
croutons and/or finely chopped parsley

Trim the parsnips at both ends and peel, then cut into approximately 5cm chunks. Chop the mushrooms roughly. Place the prepared parsnips and mushrooms in a pressure cooker or large saucepan with all the remaining ingredients. If you are using a pressure cooker, cook at pressure for 12-15 minutes. If you are using a saucepan, cover and simmer for approximately 40 minutes, stirring occasionally, until the split peas are very soft.
There is no need to puree this soup. Just mash thoroughly and serve piping hot, garnished with croutons and/or finely chopped parsley.

Don't be put off by the unusual ingredients in this soup; the result is a delightful combination of flavour and texture. As parsnips are readily available for much of the year and are not expensive, this soup can provide an economical and nutritious meal in a hurry, served with wholemeal bread, a salad and cheeses (try a port wine cheese, or other specialty types such as fruit and nut if you have guests). It can be presented in smaller portions for a lunch or an entree.

*Five spice powder is available in the gourmet spice range at supermarkets, or from oriental commodity stores. It isn't easy to reproduce, as it has a base of ground star anise, but a mixture of ground allspice and nutmeg would produce a reasonably similar taste for this dish.

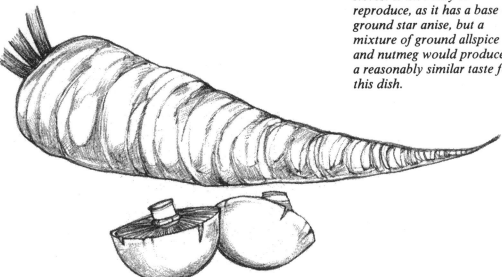

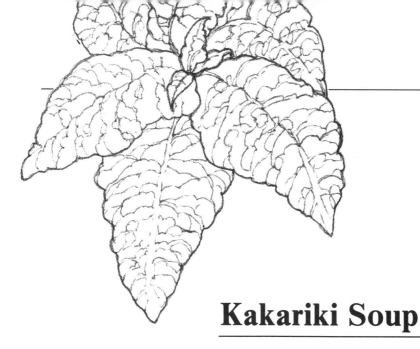

Kakariki Soup

Kakariki simply means green, which doesn't really explain much in culinary terms. If honesty were to prevail, I think that kakariki is a lovely word, and I can — at a pinch — justify its use by the fact that this soup is green (though not bright green). Anyway it's very quick to prepare — you just throw everything in a large pot or pressure cooker and cook!

It's a wonderfully tasty, nutritious and sustaining soup which provides a complete meal if served with wholemeal bread and a variety of cheeses. Try some of the speciality ones such as fruit and nut, joboe, or red and green pepper, followed by fresh fruit if you wish. This soup is also nice served in smaller amounts as an entree.

This soup may be microwaved, but there seems little advantage for this quantity. Freezes well.

600g potatoes
2 medium onions, peeled and chopped
1 cup green split peas
1 tbsp ground cumin
1 tbsp dried basil
2-2½ tsp salt
freshly ground black pepper
8 cups stock or water
300 g spinach or silver beet leaves, weighed with main stalk removed
1 tbsp lemon juice
lite sour cream or plain yoghurt as a garnish (entirely optional)

Peel the potatoes and chop into approximately 5cm cubes. Peel the onions and chop roughly. Place the potatoes and onions in a large saucepan or pressure cooker, with the split peas, cumin, basil, salt, pepper and the stock or water.
Add the roughly chopped spinach or beet leaves, cover and bring to the boil.
Turn down the heat. If you are cooking the soup in a pressure cooker, simmer for 12 minutes. If you are cooking in a saucepan, you will first need to soak the split peas in 3 cups of the stock or water measure for 8 hours. Then proceed as above, adding the remaining stock/water measure with the rest of the ingredients. Simmer for approximately 35-40 minutes, or until split peas are very soft. Stir occasionally during this time.
Remove from the heat and pour into a food processor bowl in several batches. Puree each batch until quite smooth (about 15 seconds each), then return to the saucepan. The soup can be left until just before you are ready to serve at this stage.
Add the lemon juice, then reheat. Adjust the seasoning and serve, garnished with a swirl of lite sour cream or yoghurt if you wish.

Oyster Soup Supreme

2 dozen oysters in their liquor
60g margarine or butter
1 tsp green peppercorns, brine packed or capers
3-4 cloves garlic, crushed
⅓ cup flour
¼ cup oyster liquor
¼ cup water or stock
5 cups milk
1¼ tsp salt or to taste
freshly ground black pepper
¼ tsp grated lemon rind (zest)
1 tbsp Worcester sauce
¼-½ cup lite sour cream or cream

Drain the oysters, reserving their liquid.
Melt the margarine or butter in a large saucepan over a gentle heat. Drain and mash the green peppercorns or capers thoroughly with the back of a fork, then add these with the garlic to the melted margarine. Saute for 1-2 minutes, then stir in the flour and cook for 1-2 minutes. Remove from the heat.
Mix the ¼ cup oyster liquid and water or stock together and add to the saucepan with 1 cup of the milk. Bring just to the boil, stirring all the time. Remove from the heat again and add a further 2 cups of the milk. Return to the heat and bring to the boil again, stirring, then repeat the process once more with the last 2 cups of milk. Simmer for 1-2 minutes. Remove from the heat, season with the salt and pepper and add the lemon zest, Worcester sauce and whisk in the lite sour cream, if using, or cream.
If you are preparing ahead, the soup may be left for a few hours at this stage.
Reheat the soup just before you are ready to serve it. The last step is to add the halved or quartered oysters when the soup is almost hot enough to serve. They really only need a minute or two standing time in a very hot liquid to cook through but remain tender.
Serve the soup just before it boils, garnished with parsley, garlic croutons or just as it is — heavenly!

There just *is* something special about a creamy oyster soup, especially when it can be produced at any time of the year (using fresh or frozen oysters). My husband regards himself as something of an oyster soup connoisseur. I largely ignored his advice when I was working with this soup, but must confess to feeling very pleased when it was pronounced the best he'd ever tasted!
Fresh is best, of course, but frozen oysters may be used. Few of us can afford to indulge a passion for oysters these days, but it certainly helps the justification process when you can produce an informal dinner or special lunch for 4-6 from 24 oysters.
Any cream soup is filling, and this soup is very satisfying, especially when served with crusty wholemeal bread sticks or bagels, a selection of cheeses and salad ingredients.

Children, who normally don't enjoy oysters in any form, love the flavour of this soup.

Mussels, cockles or other shellfish may be used to produce this soup, with different but very good results. Using approximate quantities, steam them open in a covered pan (3-5 minutes) with 1 cup water (discard the shells). Use ½ cup of this liquid in the soup instead of the oyster liquid/ water mixture.

Not suitable for freezing or microwaving.

Mushroom and Cauliflower Bisque

This soup is quick to prepare and is a tasty, nutritious soup with an interesting texture and a rich creamy flavour. Try it with some oysters (optional) added at the end of cooking, as a treat you can stretch. Crusty wholemeal bread sticks are a perfect complement, and the recipe provides a light meal for 4, or a starter for 6.

This soup may be microwaved, but not frozen.

250g cauliflower, cut into florets
1 large onion, peeled and chopped
2 cloves garlic, crushed
120g mushrooms, chopped
⅓ cup sour cream
¾ tsp grated lemon rind (zest)
60g margarine or butter
⅓ cup flour
2½ cups milk
¾ cup stock or water
1 tsp salt
lots of freshly ground black pepper
2 tbsp oyster liquor (optional)
12-18 chopped oysters (optional), frozen or fresh
1 dsp lemon juice
finely chopped parsley

Steam the cauliflower, onion, garlic and mushrooms in ⅓ cup water or microwave in 2 tbsp water, covered, adding the mushrooms after the other vegetables are partially cooked. Steam until just tender (about 4 minutes on high in a microwave). Drain but reserve any liquid from the cooking. Place the drained, cooked vegetables in a food processor with the sour cream, lemon rind and 1 cup of the milk measure. Blend well for about 40 seconds, until finely pureed.

Melt the margarine or butter in a medium-large saucepan over a gentle heat. Add the flour and cook, stirring, for 30 seconds, then remove from heat and whisk in the remaining 1½ cups of milk.

Return to the heat and cook, stirring, until the roux thickens, then add the stock or water made up to ¾ cup with the reserved liquid from the cooked vegetables.

Now add the pureed vegetables and bring to the boil, stirring. The soup may be left at this stage. Just before you are ready to serve, reheat almost to boiling point, and add the oyster liquor and chopped oysters if you are including them. Cook for 1 minute only. If not, proceed to the lemon juice. Stir in the juice, check the seasoning, and serve immediately in bowls garnished with chopped parsley.

Harvest Soup

1 kg pumpkin
600g fresh tomatoes, preferably, or equivalent tinned
2 medium onions, peeled and chopped
¾ cup mung beans (not sprouts)
2 bay leaves
1 tsp freshly ground black pepper
2 tsp green herb instant stock
1 tsp salt
1 tbsp fresh chopped basil leaves or 1 tsp dried
3½ cups water

Peel and chop the pumpkin into large dice and place in a large saucepan or pressure cooker. Add the chopped tomatoes, onions and all the remaining ingredients, then cover and simmer for about 40 minutes or until the pumpkin and mung beans are soft or pressure cook for 12-15 minutes. Remove the bay leaves and allow to cool for 10 minutes if you have the time, before pureeing in a food processor. Reheat and serve.

Harvest time always conjures up the reds and golds of autumn, and the colour of this soup is redolent of the season. It's a thick, substantial soup with the naturally rich flavour of pumpkin lifted by tomatoes and herbs. Serve it with slabs of wholemeal bread and a variety of cheeses, then follow it with a selection of fresh fruits. This soup appeals to all tastes and is a meal in itself.

If you are cooking in a saucepan rather than a pressure cooker, you may need to add a little more water at the end of cooking, because of the longer cooking time. About ½ cup should do, but this addition will depend on how thick you like a soup to be.

Not recommended for microwave cooking in this quantity. Freezes well.

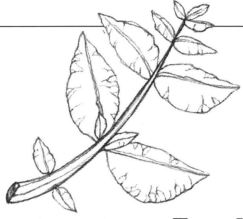

Zucchini Soup with Mint and Anchovy

If you enjoy trying something different, this soup is quite a treat. The anchovies completely fade into the background, but give the soup a boost in terms of depth or heartiness of flavour. It's simple to make, and is a meal in itself if garnished with a swirl of natural yoghurt and served with wholemeal bread.

Broccoli can be used instead of zucchini if desired.

**Thick mint sauce is readily available in bottles at supermarkets. Although this quantity sounds quite a lot, it is correct — taste as you go, if you're unsure.*

500g peeled potatoes, chopped
45g margarine or butter
1 large onion, peeled and finely chopped
4 cloves garlic, crushed
50g tin anchovy fillets, drained and mashed
5 cups vegetable stock, or water with 3 tsp instant green herb stock
500g zucchini, chopped*
½ tsp salt or to taste
1 tsp freshly ground black pepper
3½-4 tbsp thick mint sauce** (not concentrate)
1/3 cup finely chopped parsley
mint leaf garnish if desired

Prepare the potatoes, then puree raw in a food processor, using the metal chopping blade.

Heat the margarine or butter in a large heavy-bottomed saucepan, then saute the onion and garlic over a medium-low heat until the onion softens.

Add the pureed potatoes and saute 2 minutes, stirring.

Add the mashed anchovies with the stock, or water and instant stock. Cover and simmer for 20 minutes. Stir occasionally to prevent any sticking to the bottom of the saucepan.

Now puree the zucchini in the processor. Add the zucchini with the seasonings and mint sauce, then cover and simmer for 10 more minutes. Stir a couple of times.

Taste to check the seasoning, add the finely chopped parsley, then serve hot, garnished with a swirl of natural yoghurt and a mint leaf garnish if desired.

Perfect Pea Soup with Nutty Garnish

3 cups frozen peas
1¼ cups green split peas
1 large onion, peeled and chopped finely
1½ tbsp coriander
7½-8 cups water
1½ cups cauliflorets, diced
2 tsp salt
lots of freshly ground black pepper

Place all the ingredients in a pressure cooker. The smaller measure of water should be sufficient, but add the remaining ½ cup if you wish at the end of cooking time. Bring to pressure on high heat, then turn the heat down and cook for 17-20 minutes. The split peas will have 'sauced' with the cooking, but the frozen peas will still be recognisable. Check the seasoning and serve piping hot, sprinkled with the nutty garnish if you wish.

If you are planning to cook this soup in a saucepan, place the split peas in a bowl with 3 cups of the water in the morning and soak for 8 hours.
Place the split peas, the water they have been soaking in plus the remaining 5 cups (use the full amount of water with this method as some liquid escapes during cooking) into a large, heavy-bottomed saucepan. Add the remaining ingredients and simmer for approximately 1¼ hours. Stir regularly, especially towards the end of cooking time to prevent sticking.

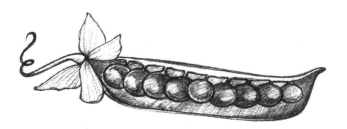

Nutty Garnish

Toast ¼ cup poppy seeds, ¼ cup pumpkin kernels and ¼ cup sunflower kernels in a heavy-bottomed pan over a gentle heat, stirring or microwave on high for 4 minutes, stirring twice during cooking time.
Store in an airtight jar.

This delicious soup has met with unqualified approval from all who have tried it. Served with wholemeal bread, it constitutes a meal in itself and is an ideal standby when time is short but a substantial meal is needed. (Cheeses are nice accompaniments, followed by fresh fruit if you wish.)

This soup can be assembled in 5 minutes and presented to the table in 25 if you have a pressure cooker. If you are using a saucepan, it will take 8 hours' soaking time, plus another hour and 20 minutes to assemble and cook.

There is no need to have any apprehension about using a pressure cooker; it is advisable to stay nearby to keep an ear open for the continual soft chuffing sound, especially when cooking split peas. These sauce down quickly, so that if the 'chuff' stops it could mean that the vent is blocked, but this is most unlikely if you haven't overfilled the cooker. Read the instructions carefully regarding its use and cleaning and you should have no trouble at all.

Not suitable for microwaving in this quantity. Freezes well.

A very nice garnish for any soup, this mixture of roasted seeds adds to both nutritional content and textural interest.

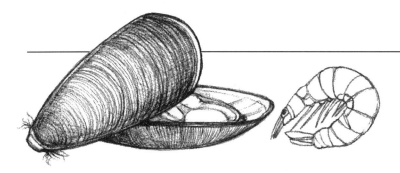

Bouillabaisse Raukawa

This wonderful seafood soup can be made very quickly, and is a meal in itself if accompanied by garlic bread, for example. Serve it with a side salad, too, if you like — lettuce, avocado and tomato tossed with a simple vinaigrette, for instance. Great for entertaining guests informally.

The mussels in this recipe are the large greenshell variety, but they could be replaced by the smaller blue mussels you can collect yourself. They must be fresh, so the shells should still be closed. (Don't panic if they open before you cook them for this recipe — they'll be all right for at least 5-6 hours, refrigerated, and will be just as succulent.)

Any firm, fresh boneless fish may be used for this soup, such as blue warehou, trevally, gemfish, lemonfish or ling.

Fish sauce (nam pla) is a sauce made from fermented fish and used as a flavouring and seasoning agent throughout Asia. It may be replaced by a slightly smaller quantity of light soya sauce, though it is worth going to some trouble to get, at any Asian specialty store.

1 tbsp oil
1 large onion, peeled and sliced thinly
3 cloves garlic, crushed (1 tsp)
1 large stalk celery, diced small
1 medium capsicum, green or red, seeded and chopped
1½ litres vegetable stock or water plus 3 tsp instant green herb stock
2 tbsp lemon juice
2½ tbsp fish sauce (nam pla)* or 1½ tbsp light soya sauce
lots of freshly ground black pepper
1 400g tin whole tomatoes, chopped, with juice or equivalent weight of fresh tomatoes, skinned and chopped
1 tbsp fresh chopped basil or oregano or 1 tsp dried
2 fresh sage leaves, chopped fine or pinch of dried
1 cup cooked rice, preferably brown
400-500g white fish fillets, chopped into approx. 5cm x 2.5cm pieces
18-24 greenshell mussels (750g-1 kg)
½-1 cup large frozen shrimps, or prawns (optional)
2 tbsp finely chopped parsley for garnish

Heat the oil in an extra large heavy-bottomed saucepan. Saute the onion and garlic for 2 minutes over a medium low heat, then add the celery and capsicum. Saute for a few more minutes.

Add the stock, lemon juice, fish sauce, pepper, chopped tomatoes and the herbs. Cover and bring to the boil, then simmer for about 12 minutes.

While this is cooking prepare the fish, scrub the mussel shells and remove the 'beards' from the mussels by pulling.

Add the cooked rice, the fish, mussels and the shrimps/ prawns if using. Bring back to the boil then simmer for another 3-4 minutes. This will give the fish time to cook and the mussels to open.

Ladle into large shallow soup bowls, sprinkled with parsley.

Turkish Carrot Soup

750g carrots
4 tbsp margarine or butter (60g)
1 tbsp ground coriander
1½ tsp salt
plenty of freshly ground black pepper
1 tsp brown sugar
3 cups water or stock
½ tsp grated whole nutmeg or ¾ tsp ground nutmeg
1 tsp grated lemon rind (zest)
½ cup plain yoghurt
extra yoghurt and chopped fresh mint leaves for garnish, plus chopped toasted almonds if desired

Carrots are both economical and versatile, and especially good with a pinch of Middle Eastern magic. This soup will provide a refreshing light lunch or entree, or the basis of a light summer meal for 4 if served with wholemeal breads, a selection of cheeses and fresh fruit. Although it is quite an unusual soup in terms of both texture and taste, it has wide appeal.

   Wash the carrots and cut off the tops and any roots — peel only if discoloured or damaged. Chop into small chunks.
Melt the butter in a medium-sized saucepan, add the coriander and saute for 1 minute. Then add the carrot chunks and saute over a moderate heat for approximately 5 minutes, stirring constantly. Add the salt, pepper, sugar, water/stock and nutmeg. Cover and simmer until tender, about 20 minutes.
Place in a food processor (you will need to do this in 2-3 lots) and process until smooth.
Return to the saucepan, add the lemon zest and the yoghurt, and whisk to combine.
Over a gentle heat, reheat almost to boiling point. Garnish with extra yoghurt and finely chopped mint. Sprinkle with finely chopped and toasted almonds if desired.

This soup may be frozen before the addition of the lemon zest and the yoghurt. May be microwaved.

31

Miso Soup

Miso is a concentrated, fermented paste made from soya beans. It is a traditional base for Japanese sauces and soups, and is a very nutritious substance — high in protein, of course, from the soya beans. Children enjoy the soup it produces, as do adults. It tastes a little like Marmite or bouillon soup, and can be made very quickly, in about 10 minutes. A tablespoon or two of miso is nice thinned with water or stock and added to stews or casseroles, stir fry meals, ordinary vegetable soup, etc. It can even be used as a spread for sandwiches, so as well as being nutritious it's very versatile.

Miso paste is available from most health food outlets and there are a number of different varieties, some light (usually called red miso), and some darker, such as barley miso and brown rice miso. The darker ones have been fermented for a longer time, and have usually been mixed with various grains. The recipe below can be used for either kind. The vegetables in the soup can be sauteed in a little oil before adding, but I find this makes very little difference to the final result.

1 medium-large onion, skinned and chopped finely
1½ tsp fresh ginger, skinned and minced finely
1½ litres water or stock (about 7 cups)
1-1½ cups finely sliced or shaved vegetables such as celery, carrot, mushroom, broccoli sprigs, cauliflower, peas (fresh or frozen), etc
3-4 tbsp miso paste — taste for preference
chopped spring onion or parsley, plus some small cubes of tofu if desired, for garnish

Place the onion and the ginger in a large saucepan with the water and bring to the boil. Simmer for a few minutes, then add the remaining vegetables. Simmer for a further 5 minutes, then remove about a cup of the water or stock. Add this to a bowl containing the miso paste and mix thoroughly. Return the miso/stock to the saucepan and reheat, without allowing it to boil again.

Ladle into bowls for serving, garnished with the chopped spring onion or parsley, and a few cubes of tofu if desired. This soup serves 4-6 adults.

Thai Soup

125g tofu, cut into 1 cm dice*
½ tsp fresh ginger, skinned and minced
1 clove garlic, crushed
3 tbsp light soya sauce

Marinate the tofu in the ingredients above to add flavour to the tofu, while you prepare the main body of the soup. Marinate in a single layer, stirring occasionally.

1 tbsp oil
1 tsp fresh ginger, skinned and minced
4 cloves garlic, crushed
½ onion, peeled and chopped finely
8 cups water
1 medium carrot, chopped into thin rounds
1 stick celery, including leaves, diced small
1 medium leek, thinly sliced or ¾ cup sliced cauliflorets
1 tbsp sugar
2½ tbsp fish sauce or 2 tbsp light soya sauce
2 tsp green herb instant stock powder
2-3 tsp miso paste
½ cup mung bean sprouts
2 lettuce or silver beet leaves (or equivalent cabbage), shredded
120g rice vermicelli or noodles, soaked in hot water for 10 minutes then drained or egg noodles, cooked until al dente then drained

Place the oil in a large saucepan and saute the ginger, garlic and onion over a gentle heat until the onion softens. Add the water, carrot, celery, leek, sugar, fish sauce, instant stock and the miso paste. Bring to the boil, then turn the heat down and simmer, covered, for 15 minutes.
Add the bean sprouts, lettuce and the rice noodles. Simmer for a further 4 minutes.
Drain the tofu, discarding the marinade, then add the tofu to the soup and cook for 1 more minute.
Serves 4-6 adults.

This simple Thai soup has a classic Eastern simplicity, although a couple of the ingredients may not be familiar to some readers. They can be replaced by more well-known ingredients, although it is nice to keep authenticity whenever possible. Fish sauce, for example, is a salting ingredient used in Asia, using fermented fish as its base rather than soya beans as in soya sauce. It really is delicious and is widely used in Thai cookery. Rice noodles (the dry white noodles you see in oriental commodity shops) are wonderful used in dishes such as this and in stir fries, etc. They taste just like conventional pasta, but you only have to soak them for 10 minutes in hot water. The actual cooking time is only 2-3 minutes after soaking, and they don't have to be boiled at all — just stir fried. They are available in many noodle widths.

This soup makes a substantial main meal, especially if served with rice as a side dish.

*You could substitute for the tofu shrimps or cubes of firm-fleshed fresh fish, in which case omit the marinating procedure.

Vegetarian

Cornmeal Roulade with Avocado and Nut Stuffing

This roulade provides a light main or lunch dish with a minimum of preparation, as the filling does not have to be pre-cooked. The recipe serves 4 hearty eaters (with crisp french bread and a tomato salad, for example, sprinkled with lemon juice, a smidgen of sugar and some finely chopped mint leaves); or 6 if served with a substantial potato dish and vegetables such as steamed broccoli, tomato halves sprinkled with herbs and seasonings and grilled, plus a green salad. (Tomatoes complement the roulade very well.)

45g margarine or butter
1/3 cup plain flour
1 cup milk
1/4 cup fine cornmeal
1/2 tsp salt
lots of freshly ground black pepper
1/2 cup finely chopped parsley
4 eggs, separated
sprinkle of poppy seeds for garnish (optional)

Filling

1 avocado, chopped
1/2 medium onion, peeled
1/2 cup pecans, chopped — walnuts may be substituted, or toasted sunflower kernels
1/4 tsp salt
freshly ground black pepper
1 tsp chilli sauce or sambal oelek
1/3 cup sour cream
1 tbsp lemon juice
1/2 cup grated parmesan cheese or tasty cheddar

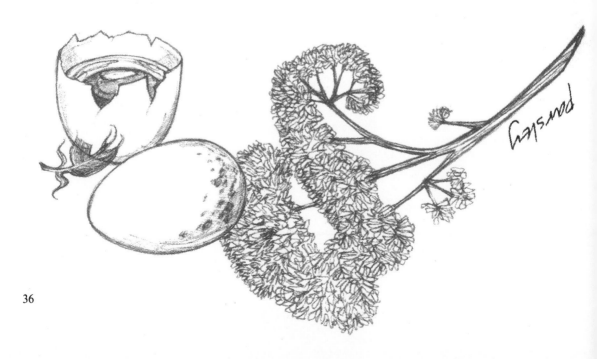

parsley

Pre-heat the oven to 180°C.

Melt the margarine or butter in a medium-sized heavy-based saucepan over a gentle heat. Stir in the flour and cook 1 minute, stirring. Remove from the heat and gradually whisk in the milk and fine cornmeal.

Cook, stirring briskly, until the mixture is smooth and thick. Remove from the heat, stir in the seasonings and parsley, then the egg yolks one at a time.

Now beat the egg whites until soft peaks form. Fold these carefully into the sauce using a metal spoon. Combine, but don't over mix.

Grease and line the bottom of a swiss roll or lamington tin with greaseproof paper. Pour the mixture evenly into this and bake at 180°C for approximately 15 minutes.

Turn out onto a tea towel and carefully remove the lining paper. Roll up into a swiss roll shape with the aid of the towel. Leave for a few minutes, then unroll again.

Peel and chop the avocado flesh. Chop the onion finely in a food processor and add to the avocado. Roughly chop the walnuts in the processor and add these to the avocado with all the remaining filling ingredients.

Sir gently to combine, then spread the roulade with the filling, leaving a narrow strip at one end so that the filling won't spill out as it cooks.

Now place the filled roulade onto an oven tray, seam side down. Sprinkle the top with poppy seeds if you wish and bake at 190°C for about 15 minutes.

The finished roulade will be golden and lightly crisped on the outside, a perfect complement to the filling.

Avocados are so superb eaten with just a sprinkle of lemon juice and seasoning, or sliced into salads, that it seems a shame to do anything else with them. When avocados are plentiful, however, this roulade is a different and tasty dish to try.

Not suitable for microwave or freezing.

Tempeh and Mushroom Filo Pie

Tempeh is not widely known in the Western world, but is now readily available from health food shops, usually vacuum packed and refrigerated. Like tofu, it is a soya bean product, but looks and tastes very different. Tempeh is made from a fermentation process which uses the whole soya bean. Its value lies in its versatility, and in the fact that it contains no chemical additives, no cholesterol, is high in protein content as well as fibre, and is a whole food. It's also the only plant food which contains Vitamin B12, which can be lacking in vegetarian diets.* This doesn't mean you have to be vegetarian to enjoy it, though. It can form the basis of delicious meals, and its other benefits make it an extremely useful addition to any diet.

On a cautionary note, tempeh doesn't look particularly appetising, nor does it taste good raw. It has a slightly sweet, nutty, cheesy taste, but when cooked has a taste and texture similar to chicken. Many people are attracted to soya bean products because of the health benefits, but genuinely dislike the actual texture of, for example, tofu. Tempeh is firmer and has a more definite taste.

*B12 is, however, found in milk and milk products.

3 tbsp margarine (45g)
1 large onion, peeled and chopped into 4
1 tsp crushed garlic (2-3 cloves)
300g tempeh, chopped into large dice
1½ cups celery, diced small
300g mushrooms, sliced
¼ cup water
1/3 cup tomato puree
2 tbsp soya sauce
freshly ground black pepper
½ tsp salt or to taste
½ cup cooked or frozen peas (optional)
1/3 cup sour cream
11 sheets of filo (phyllo) pastry
3 tbsp margarine, melted, for brushing over pastry

Pre-heat the oven to 190°C.
Melt the margarine in a large heavy-based frypan over a gentle heat. Place the onion, garlic and tempeh into a food processor and chop until the mixture resembles breadcrumbs. Saute in the margarine, stirring, for 2-3 minutes, then add the diced celery and saute for 2 minutes more, or until lightly golden.
Slice the mushrooms and add to the frypan. Now add the water, tomato puree, soya sauce, pepper, salt and peas. Cook, stirring, for about 7 minutes. (If you are using frozen peas, cook for a few minutes longer.)
Stir in the sour cream and set aside.
Butter a shallow ovenproof dish such as a small roasting or lasagne pan, about 35 x 23cm.

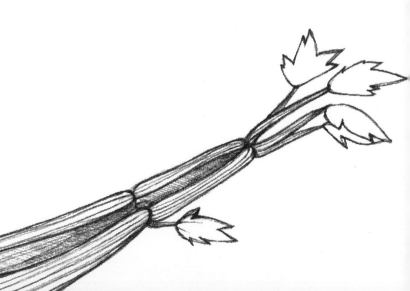

Take 11 sheets of filo pastry and cut them to size if necessary. Allow 6 sheets for the bottom of the pie and 5 for the top. The top sheets can be cut smaller than the bottom ones, which should extend up the sides as well as covering the bottom of the dish.

Take the bottom sheets first, and brush every second layer with butter. Arrange these in the prepared dish, pour in the filling and even it out. Repeat the buttering process for the top sheets, except of course that the top two sheets will be buttered.

Fold the protruding pastry sides gently over the filling, then place the topping sheets of filo over this, tucking well down the sides. Decorate with any leftover pastry pieces if desired, butter these, then make 4-5 slits in the top of the pie with a sharp knife.

Bake for 30-40 minutes at 190°C.

This pie is delicious and makes a large quantity, enough to serve 6-8 people. Serve with baked potatoes, green beans, green salad and a tomato salad, for example. A sweet fruit chutney is also a nice accompaniment.

If you want to add tempeh to a stir fry for a speedy meal, try brushing the tempeh with olive oil, then grilling it until it turns golden on both sides. Then you can crumb it in a food processor or dice it before adding it to your mixture, rather than sauteeing it first, then adding it last.

Not recommended for microwaving. May be frozen, then reheated in a hot oven.

Potato Boats

4 medium-sized potatoes, each 150-200g
a little oil and salt
1 tbsp margarine
1 tsp Marmite or other yeast extract
$^1/_3$-$^1/_2$ cup milk
$^1/_2$ cup grated cheddar cheese
1 tbsp relish or chutney (or tomato sauce)

This is my version of an old favourite. In my childhood, it was always a treat to have potato boats for tea, so I had to resurrect a memory of them for my own children. For a simple family meal, they are delicious served with just a crisp salad, of celery and apple, for example, or you can cook an omelette to accompany them if you wish. Eat them skins and all — there's no need to waste anything!
This recipe serves 4, but if you want to serve 6, simply prepare 1½ times the recipe.

Pre-heat the oven to 190°C or prick the scrubbed potatoes with a fork, then microwave on high for 8-10 minutes.
If baking, scrub the potatoes carefully, then dry them on a kitchen towel. Prick each one several times with a fork.
Brush each potato with a little cooking oil, then sprinkle over a little salt and rub this into the skins. This ensures that the potatoes will be crisp, but not too dry.
Bake at 190°C for 1 hour or until they are soft enough to be pricked easily with a fork or skewer.
Cut a top from each baked or microwaved potato and set aside.
Carefully scoop out the potato without breaking the outside skin, using a teaspoon to do this.
Mash the potato you have scooped out, then beat it with all the other ingredients until the mixture is creamy and smooth.
Now spoon the stuffing back into the potato skins and place the top back on.
Place the boats on a baking tray and bake for 25-30 minutes at 190°C or replace in a microwave oven and cook on high for about 3 minutes.

Mushroom Blues

4 medium-sized potatoes, about 140g each (560g in total approx.)
1 tsp margarine
3-4 cloves garlic, crushed
150g mushrooms, chopped
2 spring onions, chopped small
½ tsp instant mushroom stock
½ cup lite sour cream
¹/3 cup grated or crumbled blue vein cheese
2 tbsp milk

Either bake the potatoes according to the instructions given on p.40 or microwave the scrubbed, dried and pricked potatoes on high for 8-10 minutes.
While the potatoes are cooking, melt the margarine in a small pan over a gentle heat and saute the garlic and mushrooms for several minutes. Add the spring onions and saute gently, until the juices from the mushrooms appear. Remove from the heat and set aside.
When the potatoes are cooked, scoop out the flesh as detailed above. Add the stock, sour cream, blue cheese and milk to the potatoes and whip until creamy and smooth with a fork.
Now add the mushroom mixture, including any juices, and combine well.
Pile the filling back into the potato shells, replace the top, and reheat as outlined above, for the Potato Boats.

Although some adults (like me) will enjoy Potato Boats, it's nice to have an alternative. Mushroom Blues are a sophisticated version of potato boats, ideal for a quick and tasty meal.

Potato Boats and Mushroom Blues freeze well to reheat. Microwave from frozen or place in hot oven.

Super Simple Souffle

This souffle is not intended to be a cordon bleu presentation, but it *is* a quick, easy and tasty dish which really can't go wrong and is always popular. Try it for lunch, served with crusty french bread and a salad, or as a light meal served with baked potatoes cooked alongside the souffle, some steamed or microwaved broccoli, or a ratatouille, and a green salad garnished with tomato wedges.

The eggs used in a souffle should always be at room temperature.

Not recommended for microwaving or freezing.

2 cups light wholemeal fresh breadcrumbs (3 medium slices)
1¾ cups hot milk
½ tsp salt
freshly ground black pepper
150g grated tasty cheddar cheese
½ cup cottage cheese
4 eggs, separated
chopped parsley for garnish

Pre-heat the oven to 200°C.
Crumb the bread in a processor, then soak in the hot milk for a couple of minutes. Stir in the seasonings and cheeses.
Separate the eggs, whisk the yolks lightly and stir in.
Beat the egg whites until stiff peaks form, then fold these gently but thoroughly into the mixture until just combined.
Pour the mixture into a greased 1-litre souffle dish, then sit in an oven pan containing 5-6cm of hot water. Bake at 200°C for 45-50 minutes. The top should be quite firm at this stage, but it needs this cooking time to ensure that the souffle is cooked through to the middle.
Garnish with the chopped parsley and serve.

Asparagus Strudel

500g thin asparagus, blanched, drained and dried well
$1/3$ cup ricotta, preferably, or cottage cheese*
$1/3$ cup cream cheese
125g chevre salade cheese, grated (a mild fetta could be substituted)
1 egg yolk
3 tbsp fresh chives, chopped fine
3 tbsp fresh dill, chopped fine
salt and freshly ground pepper
8 sheets filo pastry
melted butter
2 tbsp grated parmesan cheese (preferably fresh)
1 small or $1/2$ large red capsicum, thinly sliced

This strudel is a delight and its interesting combination of flavours/textures will be enjoyed by guests and family, including children.

* Use ricotta in preference to cottage cheese if it is available. If you do use cottage cheese, however, beat or process it to remove any lumps. Alternatively, you could happily use $2/3$ cup ricotta instead of the combination of ricotta/cream cheese.

Mix the ricotta, cream cheese, chevre, yolk, herbs and season well with salt and pepper.

Lie one sheet of filo pastry, long side towards you, on your bench. Brush with melted butter, then place another sheet of filo on top.

Repeat so that you have 4 sheets, sprinkling with the parmesan between the 3rd and 4th sheets.

Now spread the ricotta mix in a strip about 7.5 cm wide (3 inches) along the long edge nearest you, leaving a 3 cm strip on both short edges for turning in as you roll the strudel up in a cylinder shape.

Arrange half the blanched, dried asparagus evenly on top of the ricotta mixture, then half the red capsicum strips on top of this. Fold in the edges and roll up.

Place the strudel onto a lightly greased or sprayed oven tray, seam side down, and make 3 small slashes using a utility knife or similar in the top of the roll.

Brush the top and sides with butter and repeat the process so that you have two strudels to cook.

Bake in a preheated oven at 180° C for 25 minutes.

Slice each roll into 4–6 pieces, garnish and serve immediately. Serves 4–6 as a main.

Kumara, Sprout and Orange Salad

This refreshing salad has many uses. It can be prepared in advance, and although the blend of mellow and sharp ingredients sounds unusual, it is most effective.

This salad can form the basis of a light meal on its own, served with breads, cheeses and fruits. It also complements the Nutty Spinach Loaf beautifully (see p.45).

500g kumara
2 oranges
½ onion, peeled and sliced thinly
½ cup sprouted chickpeas or other sprouts (alfalfa, mung, blue pea, etc.)
¼ cup oil
¾-1 tsp salt
lots of freshly ground black pepper
½ tsp cumin
½ tsp turmeric
2 tbsp lemon juice or cider vinegar
2 tbsp finely chopped parsley

Peel the kumara and chop into approximately even sizes so that they cook at the same time. Place in some boiling, salted water until just tender — don't overcook. Drain well, slice and place in a serving bowl.

Peel the oranges and chop into 2-3cm pieces. Slice the onion thinly.

Add the oranges, onion and the chickpeas or other sprouts to the kumara.

Place the oil, salt, pepper, cumin, turmeric, lemon juice and parsley in a screw-top jar and shake well.

Pour over the kumara and other ingredients in the bowl and toss lightly (the kumara should still be warm).

Cover and chill until serving time. Toss again just before serving.

Nutty Spinach Loaf

300g spinach or silver beet leaves, weighed without white stalk
1 large onion, peeled and chopped
1 cup roasted peanuts*
1½ cups fresh wholemeal breadcrumbs (about 2½ medium slices)
2 eggs
¾-1 tsp salt
lots of freshly ground black pepper
1 tsp chopped fresh sage leaves or ½ tsp dried
½ cup plain yoghurt
1 tbsp soya sauce
1 cup grated fetta cheese
tomato wedges and parsley to garnish

Pre-heat the oven to 190°C.
Wash the spinach or silver beet, shake off excess water, then remove the central rib from the leaves and weigh.
Chop roughly, then place with the onion in a plastic bowl if microwaving (4 minutes on high) or a saucepan (7 minutes over a gentle heat). Add no extra water for either method, but if cooking in a saucepan, shake once or twice. Cook, covered, for the times specified. Uncover and set aside to cool.

Finely chop the roasted peanuts in a food processor, then turn out into a medium-large bowl.
Now crumb the bread in the processor and add to the chopped peanuts.
Break the eggs into the processor bowl, then add the cooked spinach or silver beet leaves and onion, salt, pepper, sage, yoghurt and the soya sauce. Process for about 30 seconds or until well combined. Pour this into the bowl with the other ingredients, then add the grated fetta cheese and stir to combine all the ingredients together thoroughly.
Grease and line the bottom of a loaf tin with greaseproof paper. Pour the loaf mixture evenly into the tin, using a spatula as you would for a cake mixture.
Bake at 190°C for 40-45 minutes, or until the centre feels firm to the touch.
Invert onto a plate and remove the lining paper. Then garnish with thinly sliced tomato wedges if you wish, and a sprinkle of finely chopped parsley.

This loaf is a favourite dish as, unlike some nutty vegetarian loaves I have tasted, it is neither dry nor bland. Lightly thickened, sauteed mushrooms could be served as a sauce to accompany it, but this really isn't necessary — it's delicious as it is.
One suggestion, though — it is very nice served with the Kumara, Sprout and Orange Salad (p.44), plus a simple green salad for an elegantly casual lunch or light dinner for 4 (6 if you add more vegetable dishes, or courses).

*The easiest way to roast raw peanuts is to microwave them on high for 5 minutes, stirring twice (6 minutes for 2 cups peanuts). You can either dry roast or, if you prefer, add ½ tsp oil to every cup of peanuts.

The fetta cheese may be replaced by tasty cheddar, or half cheddar and half cottage cheese, but do use fetta if you can; it adds a wonderful flavour to this loaf (relatively low in fat, too).

Not recommended for microwaving, but may be frozen.

Blue Vegetable and Filo Pie

This pie is delicious, economical, and has a delightful combination of flavours. I've served it to people who normally dislike blue vein cheese and to their astonishment, they've loved this pie so much that they've wanted the recipe themselves.

You could change slightly the proportion of vegetables used, but this combination seems to work best for taste. Pop some potatoes into the oven to bake before you start preparing the pie. Then you need only a fresh green salad garnished with bean sprouts and tomato wedges to complete the meal.

Not suitable for freezing or microwaving.

2 tbsp oil
2 medium-large onions, peeled and chopped
3 cloves garlic, crushed
350g cauliflorets, sliced thin, then chopped in half
450g zucchini, sliced
1 cup shredded silver beet or spinach leaves, packed
2 medium tomatoes, chopped
1 cup cottage cheese
½ cup sour cream
¼ cup burghul (bulghar) or dry breadcrumbs
80-90g blue vein cheese, grated or crumbled (about ½ cup)
½ cup chopped walnuts
1 tsp salt
freshly ground black pepper
6 full sheets filo (phyllo) pastry
2½ tbsp margarine or butter, melted

Pre-heat the oven to 190°C.
Heat the oil in a large pan over a gentle heat. Saute the onions and garlic until the onions soften, then add the prepared cauliflorets and zucchini. Saute gently for 5-7 minutes, until the cauliflower is still crisp, and almost cooked. Add the shredded silver beet or spinach and chopped tomatoes and cook for another 2-3 minutes.
Remove from the heat and transfer the cooked vegetables to a large bowl. Stir in the remaining ingredients and combine thoroughly.
Grease a shallow rectangular baking dish — one measuring 30 x 20 cm is ideal. Melt the margarine.
Lay out 2 sheets of filo on your bench top and brush lightly with some of the melted butter. Place another 2 sheets on top of the first two, and brush with butter. Place another 2 sheets on top of these so that you have 6 sheets. Don't brush with butter this time.
Cut the sheets in half lengthways (providing you are using a dish of the approximate size specified); then lift one of the 2 piles (6 of the half-sheets) into the dish. They should cover the bottom of the dish and come part way up the sides, though this is not vital. Pour the filling into the pie and spread out evenly.
Now lift the remaining 6 half-sheets to fit over the filling. Tuck the overlap down the sides of the filling to contain it in a pie shape, then make several small gashes with a knife in the top pastry.
Brush the entire top thoroughly with melted butter.
Bake at 190°C for approximately 40 minutes.

Zucchini Dash

900g zucchini
500g fresh ripe tomatoes, or equivalent tinned (drained)
2 tbsp oil
1 medium onion, peeled and sliced finely
3 cloves garlic, crushed
3 tbsp wine vinegar
1¹/₂ tbsp sugar
1 tbsp soya sauce
1 tsp salt
lots of freshly ground black pepper
1 cup tinned or cooked chickpeas (optional)
2 tbsp basil pesto or ¹/₃ cup finely chopped fresh basil
60g crumbled fetta cheese
¹/₂ cup sliced black olives

This dish is very quick to make and can be served hot, warm or at room temperature — over steamed rice (white or brown), stuffed into pita bread or with baked potatoes. It is tasty, nutritious and a recipe that everyone will enjoy.

Chop the zucchini into large dice and chop the tomatoes (it is not necessary to blanch and peel the tomatoes although it is preferable).
Heat the oil in a medium sized heavy based frypan.
Add the onion and garlic, then saute over a gentle heat until the onion softens.
Add the prepared zucchini and saute, stirring regularly, for about 3 minutes.
Now add the chopped tomatoes, vinegar, sugar, soya sauce, salt and pepper.
Simmer, uncovered, stirring regularly, for 10–15 minutes.
Add the chickpeas if using, then the basil pesto or fresh basil and heat through.
Transfer the mixture to a heated serving dish.
Garnish with the crumbled fetta and olives, and serve.

chives

Summer Zucchini and Nut Fritters with Tomato and Caper Sauce

The summer catch cry for home gardeners seems to be 'Help! What do I do with rioting zucchini?' These fritters are ideal for a quick meal as they are tasty, no fuss but quite substantial. They can be served without the sauce, but this is also very simply made and provides balance and eye appeal.

Serve with pasta tossed with just a little heated cream or yoghurt and seasonings (or Creamy Herbed Pasta p.72), lightly steamed broccoli and/or a large green salad. Serves 4-6.

*Raw peanuts may be roasted in a microwave — add 1 tsp oil and a small amount of salt if desired. Cook 5 minutes on high, stirring twice.

These fritters are not recommended for microwave cooking. They may be frozen, then reheated in a hot oven or in a microwave, but they are best eaten as soon as they are cooked.

4 cups grated zucchini (about 4 zucchini)
3-4 cloves garlic, crushed
1 tbsp fresh basil or oregano, finely chopped or 1 tsp dried
2 tbsp finely chopped chives
1 cup plain flour
2 tsp baking powder
1 cup chopped roasted peanuts*
4 eggs
1 generous tsp green herb instant stock
freshly ground black pepper
½ cup cottage cheese
1 tbsp lemon juice
1/3 cup sour cream

Grate the zucchini and place in a large bowl with the garlic, basil or oregano, chives, flour and baking powder. Chop the roasted peanuts in a processor and add to the other ingredients in the bowl.

Break the eggs into another bowl with the remaining ingredients and whisk vigorously. Add to the zucchini and dry ingredients and mix thoroughly with a large spoon until well combined.

Heat 3-4 tbsp oil in a heavy-based frypan at medium heat, then drop spoonfuls of the fritter mixture into the hot oil. Cook 3-4 minutes on each side, until golden brown. Take care that the heat is not too high, to ensure that the centre of the fritters cook as well as the outside. You will probably have to cook this mixture in 2 or 3 batches. As each batch cooks, drain on absorbent paper, add more oil to the pan as required and keep the cooked fritters warm until ready to serve.

Tomato and Caper Sauce

1 tbsp oil
1 onion, skinned and chopped finely
2 cloves garlic, crushed
1 small capsicum, seeded and chopped
1 440g tin tomato puree
1 tsp capers, chopped
½ tsp salt
freshly ground black pepper

   Heat the oil in a small heavy-based saucepan. Saute the
onion, garlic and capsicum over a low heat until the onion
softens.
Add the tomato puree, the capers and seasonings, then
simmer for 10 minutes.
Serve in a jug or bowl to accompany the fritters.

Curried Pumpkin Frittata

Frittatas are very simple dishes, quick to prepare and very popular. These frittatas can be served as a one-dish meal, with a salad; or you could serve with extra cooked vegetables if you wish.

2 tbsp oil
2 onions, peeled and sliced thinly
2 cloves garlic, crushed
1 capsicum, seeded and sliced
2 tsp good quality curry powder
600g peeled pumpkin, sliced thinly into 5 x 2.5cm pieces
2 medium potatoes, peeled and sliced thinly
½ tsp chilli powder (less if you wish)
1 tsp instant green herb stock
½ tsp salt
lots of freshly ground black pepper
1½ cups broccoli sliced, including stalks or zucchini
3 tomatoes, fresh or tinned, chopped
1 tbsp fresh chopped oregano or 1 tsp dried or 1 tsp fresh chopped thyme or ½ tsp dried

Heat the oil in a large heavy-based frypan with a lid, then saute the onions and garlic over a medium-low heat. Add the capsicum and curry powder and saute for 1-2 minutes, then add the pumpkin and potatoes. Stir to combine, then cover and simmer over a low heat for 20-25 minutes, stirring 3-4 times. The potatoes and pumpkin should be just cooked at this stage.
Now add the broccoli, the tomatoes and the herbs and mix gently. Place the lid on again and cook for another 10 minutes, stirring once.
Pour on the prepared topping (below) and cook for another 3-4 minutes, uncovered, tipping the pan so that the topping covers the vegetables as evenly as possible. Don't stir once you have poured on the topping. Traditionally, you should place the pan under a grill until the topping is cooked. Grilling is actually preferable, as the topping puffs up and turns golden brown, but sometimes this is not practicable as the siting of oven grills vary, and the dish you cook the frittata in will have to be quite large — there may not be room under some of the modern grills.

Topping
4 large eggs
200g soft or silken tofu (not extra firm)
1 cup grated tasty cheese or mozzarella
1 tsp salt
freshly ground black pepper

Place the topping ingredients in a food processor and blend until well combined. Proceed as outlined above.

Potato Masala

4 tbsp oil
1 tsp cumin seeds
1 large onion, peeled and finely diced
$^1/_2$ tsp turmeric
1 tsp ground coriander
1 tsp ground cumin

$^1/_4$-$^1/_2$ tsp chilli powder
2 tsp tomato concentrate
175 ml water (reduce if extending recipe) — water should not cover potatoes
4-5 large potatoes, peeled and cubed — 1kg unpeeled weight
$^1/_4$ small cauliflower, cut into small florets
$^1/_2$-$^3/_4$ cup frozen peas
$^1/_2$ tsp garum masala
1-2 fresh chillies, seeded and chopped fine
1 tsp salt
1 tbsp chopped coriander leaves (optional)

Heat the oil in a large saucepan, electric frypan or similar. Add the cumin seeds and turn heat down when they start to 'pop'.
Add the finely diced onion and saute until soft, then the turmeric, coriander, cumin and chilli powder. Stir 2–3 minutes, then add the tomato concentrate.
Now add the water and the cubed potatoes.
Bring to the boil, turn down the heat, cover and simmer until the potatoes are half cooked, about 10–15 minutes.
Add the prepared cauliflower and simmer, uncovered and stirring regularly, until the potatoes are cooked — about another 10 minutes.
Stir in the frozen peas, garum masala, fresh chillies and salt.
Cook for 5 minutes more. Stir in or garnish with the fresh coriander leaves to serve (if using).

This dish can anchor a simple Indian meal on its own — or it can be one of several curries forming a more elaborate Indian style feast. Either way, it is especially tasty and nutritious served with a dhal such as the one on p 66; rice, chutneys, raitas such as a simple plain yoghurt and grape dish, and unleavened bread such as chapati.

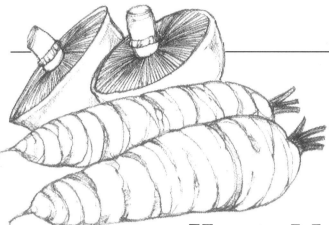

Hearty Mushroom Sauce

This very quick mushroom sauce is a good standby when you have little time to cook. It tastes good, it's satisfying and it's so quick to prepare.

Try it served over steamed savoury burghul (bulghar) or kibbled wheat (see next page) or steamed brown rice, accompanied by lightly steamed or microwaved broccoli; corn cobs or baked/steamed pumpkin; plus a green salad of shredded lettuce, sprouted chickpeas, sliced cucumber and fresh tomatoes.

Suitable for microwaving and freezing.

*There are many different kinds of miso (a paste made from fermented soya beans, sometimes combined with various grains). Hatcho or red miso have not been aged as long as other miso pastes, so they have a lighter flavour. You could replace the miso with 1-2 tsp yeast extract such as Marmite, plus a dash of soya sauce, but do try some miso if possible — apart from the nutritional value, it has its own unique taste.

1 tbsp margarine or butter
½ medium onion, peeled and sliced thinly
2 cloves garlic, crushed
1 tsp fresh ginger, grated or minced
1 medium carrot, diced small
1 small capsicum, green or red, seeded and diced small
1 stalk celery, diced small
250-300g fresh mushrooms, chopped
½ cup tomato puree
2 tsp miso, hatcho or red,* or yeast extract such as Marmite
¾ cup water
¼ tsp salt or to taste
freshly ground pepper
chopped parsley to garnish

Melt the margarine or butter in a heavy-bottomed saucepan over a medium-low heat. Saute the onion, garlic, ginger and carrot, stirring, until the onion softens.
Add the diced capsicum and celery and saute for 3 minutes, stirring. Now add the chopped mushrooms. Cook for another 2-3 minutes, stirring, until the mushrooms start to cook down.
Add the tomato puree. Mix the miso with a little water until smooth, then add to the saucepan with the water measure and seasonings.
Simmer uncovered, stirring regularly, for 5 minutes.
Garnish with the parsley and serve.

Steamed Savoury Burghul

1 tbsp olive oil
1 medium onion, peeled and chopped finely
1½ cups burghul or kibbled wheat
2¼ cups water or stock
salt and freshly ground black pepper to season
fresh parsley to garnish

Heat the oil in a heavy-based pan or saucepan over a moderate heat.
Saute the onion and burghul or kibbled wheat until the wheat smells lightly toasted, about 5 minutes, stirring constantly.
Add the water or stock, cover and reduce heat to low.
Cook until the liquid has been absorbed and the grain is soft — about 15-20 minutes for burghul, 25 minutes for kibbled wheat. Check a couple of times during cooking to ensure that the burghul is cooking, but that it is not cooking too fast.
Stir and add seasoning to taste.
Garnish with parsley and serve immediately.

Burghul (bulghar) is more commonly known as the base ingredient of tabouleh, the popular Middle Eastern salad.
This recipe is intended to complement the Hearty Mushroom Sauce (previous page). It's a nice alternative to rice on occasion — and it cooks more quickly for this recipe. Kibbled wheat may be substituted for the burghul, needing only a slightly longer cooking time.

May be microwave cooked, but there seems little advantage for this dish. Not suitable for freezing.

Arabian Risotto

Grains and pulses together provide high quality protein, and all cultures have ways of combining the two — for example, baked beans on toast in our culture. This nutritious risotto is a quick, one-dish meal which is popular with everyone. Try it garnished with plain yoghurt, accompanied by steamed, microwaved or baked pumpkin/corn cobs and a green salad garnished with tomato segments.

2 tbsp oil
2 cloves garlic, crushed
1 onion, skinned and chopped finely
1½ cups brown rice
½ cup brown lentils
4 cups water
2-3 tbsp lemon juice or wine vinegar
2 tsp green herb instant stock
salt and pepper to taste
4-5 silver beet leaves, shredded
½ cup chopped mushrooms (optional)
½ cup pine nuts
sambal oelek or other chilli condiment garnish if desired

Heat the oil in a large heavy-based frypan and saute the onion and garlic until soft. Add rice and lentils, stirring, until coated with oil.

Add 2 cups of the water and bring to the boil. Reduce the heat and simmer, uncovered, for 15 minutes.

Now add the remaining 2 cups of water with the stock and the lemon juice.

Cover and simmer for 20 minutes or until the rice and lentils are tender and the water is absorbed.

Add the silver beet, mushrooms if you are including them, and pine nuts.

Cook, stirring, for about 4 minutes more or until the silver beet is tender. Season to taste with salt and freshly ground black pepper.

Allow each individual to help themselves to the chilli condiment if they wish.

Satay Stir Fry

The vegetables given here may be substituted for others or the quantities varied — you need about 9 cups vegetables for 6 serves — but *do* include the sprouted beans, as these boost the protein content, or add some small cubes of tofu or nuts at the end of cooking. Try your own variations with this meal — you can use fewer vegetables, for example, and substitute cooked noodles instead.

2 tbsp oil
1 large onion, peeled and chopped finely
2 cloves garlic, crushed
2½–3 tbsp satay paste*
1 medium carrot, cut into julienne sticks
1 small capsicum, seeded and sliced
2 celery stalks, sliced diagonally (2 cups)
2 cups cauliflorets, sliced thinly
3-4 zucchini, sliced diagonally (2 cups)
2 cups broccoli florets, sliced thinly
1 cup sprouted chickpeas or other sprouts such as mung beans
1 tbsp soya sauce
¼-⅓ cup stock or water

Heat the oil in a wok or large frypan over a gentle heat and saute the onion and garlic until soft.
Stir in the satay paste until it is smooth, then add the carrot sticks and saute for 1 minute. If you are preparing ahead, you can just stir in the carrot, remove from the heat and leave until the final minutes before you want to serve the meal.
Turn the heat to medium and add all the remaining vegetables. Stir fry for about 2-3 minutes, taking care not to burn them, then add the soya sauce and water and saute for approximately 4 minutes more. At this stage the vegetables should taste tender-crisp, subtly flavoured with satay and retain their bright colours.
Serve immediately.

This stir fry is a very simple, quick and easy meal in one dish. It can be served simply with plain steamed rice; it also complements sushi (p.58) very well.

I'm always wary of using ingredients which sound too unusual or hard to find, but I have to make an exception in this case. The satay paste (not sauce) used in this dish is a Chinese condiment, readily available at specialty stores, and one which is wonderful to have on hand as it means you can create an infinite variety of quick, flavourful stir fry meals which, incidentally, both adults and children will enjoy. A very thick, dark brown paste with a nut kernel and sesame base, it keeps indefinitely in the refrigerator after opening. It can most readily be bought in a glass jar with a red plastic screw-on top (not to be confused with the range of sate sauces available in a range of tins, bottles and jars).

Not suitable for microwaving or freezing.

Indonesian Stir-Fried Vegetable Curry

A curry stir fry seems almost a contradiction in terms, as most good curries need at least 20-30 minutes' cooking time; the spices need time to percolate through and flavour the dish in the traditionally accepted manner.

This dish circumvents that procedure, as a curry paste is prepared first. Thus the vegetables retain their colour and crispness, the curry paste has a mild depth of flavour, rather than the harsh taste you might expect from a quick curry, and a touch of coconut cream adds its own special taste.

My good friend and partner in The Vegetarian Adventure Cook Book, *Sue Carruthers, gave me the basis for this recipe. After about 4 adaptations, I hope the result is as she intended it to be. It's now a favourite of mine — and it's so quick to prepare, with the curry paste already made. Not only that, but everyone loves it!*

Serve over steamed long grain or glutinous rice, a dhal if you wish, a green salad and some sambals and raitas (p.100) or for a more casual meal, just serve the stir fry with the rice and a salad.

Curry Paste
3 tbsp ghee or clarified butter (or oil)
1 tsp mustard seeds
2 medium onions, peeled and chopped finely
3 cloves garlic, crushed
2 tsp coriander
2 tsp cumin
2 tsp tumeric
½ tsp chilli powder
¼ tsp cinnamon
¼ tsp fenugreek
1 tsp freshly ground black pepper
1 tsp salt
1 400g tin whole tomatoes, chopped, with juice

Melt the ghee or clarified butter in a heavy-bottomed saucepan.
Over a medium-high heat, saute the mustard seeds until they 'pop', then turn the heat down immediately.
Add the onions and garlic. Saute these over a low heat until the onion softens. Take care not to burn.
Now add all the spices and seasonings, saute for about 3 minutes, then add the tomatoes and juice.
Bring the mixture to the boil, then simmer uncovered for 25-30 minutes. The paste should be well reduced by this stage, and thickened. In the later stages of cooking, of course, it needs more regular stirring to ensure that it doesn't stick.
Allow the paste to cool, then place in a jar with a lid and keep in the refrigerator for up to 3 weeks, or freeze. This quantity of paste should produce enough for 4-5 curries, so if you want to freeze it, try dividing it into 4 tbsp lots, sufficient for 1 curry each.

Having made the curry paste (above) it's a very simple matter to actually produce the meal. Serve it with steamed white or brown rice, though steamed white glutinous rice is preferable.* Add a baked banana or two (baked or microwaved in their pricked skins) a raita and some sambals including a fresh tomato sambal (p.100), some chutneys and extra nuts.

This recipe calls for 8 cups of mixed chopped or sliced vegetables. I have given suggestions here, but this requirement is infinitely variable and you could use whatever fresh vegetables you have on hand. Half a cup of finely sliced tofu could also be added as part of or extra to this measure, in the last 2 minutes of cooking.

2 tbsp oil
1 large onion, peeled and sliced finely (this is not part of the 8-cup measure)
2 capsicums, green or red, seeded and chopped (1½ cups)
1½ cups sliced zucchini or celery
2 cups sliced mushrooms
1 cup snow peas, sliced or green beans
1 cup cauliflorets, sliced
1 cup broccoli florets, sliced
4 tbsp prepared curry paste (above)
1 tbsp light soya sauce
1 tsp sambal oelek or chilli sauce
1 tbsp peanut butter
1 tbsp fish sauce (nam pla) preferably or 2 tsp light soya sauce
¼ cup water
½ cup tinned coconut cream
½ cup slivered almonds or blanched whole almonds

This dish cooks very quickly, so prepare the vegetables, and mix the soya sauce, sambal oelek, peanut butter and fish sauce together before you begin.
Heat the oil over a medium heat in a wok or large heavy-based frypan. Quickly saute the onion until it softens, then stir in the 8 cups of prepared vegetables. Saute these, stirring constantly, for 5 minutes.
Stir in the curry paste and the remaining ingredients apart from the almonds. Saute for another 2 minutes.
Pile onto a warm serving dish if desired. Sprinkle the almonds over the top as a garnish, and serve.

Glutinous rice ('sticky') is commonly eaten in Asia and has a delightful flavour and texture. It is a dry but sticky rice which is cooked in the same way but for a little longer than ordinary long grain. It microwaves beautifully (cold water 2.5 cm above the level of rice, cover, then microwave for 21 minutes on high). This is 1 minute longer than for ordinary long grain.

Sushi with Dipping Sauce

Sushi is very popular as cocktail finger food, or for serving as part of a Japanese meal, as an accompaniment to an Asian soup or ethnic lunch.

1½ cups short grain rice
2½-3 cups water
⅓ cup white wine vinegar
2 tbsp sugar
1 tbsp salt
4 sheets nori (dried seaweed sheets)
thin sticks of raw carrot, gherkin, cucumber or capsicum
thin slices of cooked omelette or sliced smoked salmon

Place the rice in a dish suitable for microwaving (straight sided glass is best) or in a saucepan.

Cover with the water — it should come to about 2.5 cm above the level of the rice, whatever cooking method you use.

If microwaving, cover the bowl with plastic wrap and microwave on high for 20 minutes. If cooking in a saucepan, place the lid on, bring to the boil then turn the heat down to very low (almost off) and steam through for 25–30 minutes.

While the rice is cooking, mix the vinegar, sugar and salt together.

As soon as the rice is cooked, stir in the vinegar mixture with a fork and turnout into a heatproof pan such as a roasting pan. Fluff again with a fork to cool as quickly as possible then leave for approximately 30 minutes.

Lie the nori long side towards you and rougher side up.

Using a flat bladed knife, spread the rice mixture onto the sheets of nori about 1cm deep, leaving a strip about 1cm wide along the side farthest away from you.

Lie 2–4 fillings along the side nearest to you, about 1 cm in from the edge, then roll up firmly but gently.

Slice the two end pieces off as they are likely to be a little ragged, then slice the roll into eight even rounds. A small, sharp knife is best for this.

Yield = 30 sushi approximately

Present on a serving plate with a small bowl of the dipping sauce and garnished with spring onion curls or some fresh chives.

Jill's Dipping Sauce

75ml white wine
1 tsp sesame oil
3 tsp peeled and finely chopped ginger
3 tsp sweet chilli sauce
150 ml soya sauce (preferably dark)
1 tsp ground coriander
2 tsp horseradish sauce
2-3 tsp honey

    Warm slightly to combine, allow to cool and keep refrigerated. This sauce can be halved, but will keep for several weeks in the refrigerator.

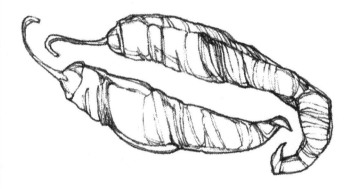

Thai Pecan or Walnut Ring with Spicy Sauce

This nut dish is simple to make, and popular with adults and children alike. The crowning touch is the sauce, but children may prefer their favourite tomato sauce as an alternative, as this sauce is quite definitely piquant. In view of this, it's probably best to serve the sauce separately if the dish is intended for a family meal. If not, however, pour this superb sauce over the ring just before serving and garnish with some extra nuts.

Suitable accompaniments would be baked potatoes and a large green salad, or lightly steamed/microwaved carrots and zucchini or cauliflower.

Either pecans or walnuts can be used; both are good, and similar, although the pecans have a smoother, richer flavour. They also cost more, however, a consideration which may be taken into account. (Do check to ensure that the nuts you buy taste fresh. Rancid nuts are guaranteed to spoil any dish.)

Can be microwave cooked or reheated, and is also delicious cold. Freezes well.

1½ cups fresh wholemeal breadcrumbs (about 3 medium slices)
1½ cups walnuts or pecans
1 onion, skinned and chopped finely
2 cloves garlic, peeled and crushed
1 tsp oil
1 medium-large carrot, cut into quarters
1 tbsp fresh parsley
2 eggs
1/3-½ cup vegetable stock or water
1½ cups cooked (or tinned) soya beans, chickpeas or lima beans
1 tsp cumin
1 tsp salt
2 tsp freshly ground black pepper
1 tbsp fish sauce, preferably or light soya

Pre-heat the oven to 180°C.
Crumb the bread in a food processor, then add the walnuts or pecans and chop small. Remove and set aside.
Saute the onion and garlic in a pan or microwave (2 minutes) with the oil until the onion softens. Place in the food processor bowl with the carrot and parsley and chop small. Add all the remaining ingredients to the processor bowl, including the breadcrumbs and nuts, and process until well mixed. A family-sized processor will handle this amount, but the mixture may have to be divided into 2 lots if you have a smaller one.
Grease the bottom and sides of a 20 cm ring tin, then line the bottom with greaseproof paper.
Pour the prepared mixture evenly into the ring tin, smoothing the top with a spatula.
Bake at 180°C for approximately 45 minutes, or until the ring is firm to the touch and a skewer inserted is clean.
Invert onto a serving plate and remove the lining paper.

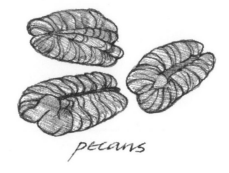

pecans

Spicy Sauce

1 tbsp oil
1 onion, peeled and chopped finely
2 cloves garlic, crushed
2 small dried red chillies, minced with a knife
¼ cup fruit chutney*
1 tsp grated orange rind (zest)
1 tbsp fresh orange juice
1 tsp grated lemon rind (zest)
1 tbsp lemon juice
1 tsp miso (red or hatcho) or yeast extract such as Marmite
1 tbsp brown sugar
1½ cups vegetable stock or water
salt to taste
freshly ground black pepper
1 tbsp cornflour mixed with 2 tbsp water
fresh coriander and extra chopped nuts for garnish

Heat the oil over a low heat in a medium saucepan, then saute the onion, garlic and chillies, stirring, until the onion softens.
Stir in the chutney, orange and lemon rinds and juices, the miso mixed to a paste with a little water, sugar, stock and seasonings.
Simmer over a medium-low heat for 10 minutes, then stir in the cornflour/water mix. Bring back to simmer, then remove from heat and pour over the nut ring. Garnish with extra chopped nuts and a little fresh coriander if you have it.

The flavour of the sauce will vary a little depending on the chutney you use. A favourite is nectarine chutney, based on a recipe for mango (p.114). Don't use tomato, for example, but peach or similar would be fine. If the chutney you use has chillies in it, you may want to reduce or omit the chillies in the sauce itself.

Suitable accompaniments are baked potatoes and a large green salad or lightly steamed or microwaved carrots and zucchini.

Burmese Nut Casserole

Although this casserole requires quite a list of individual ingredients, it is nevertheless quickly prepared. Raw peanuts are delicious in a dish such as this, as they don't soften or 'mush'. Peanuts, of course, are not a nut but a legume, so if you serve this casserole with rice or with pasta (especially brown rice or wholemeal pasta), you are consuming good quality protein. Nutritional matters aside, however, this is a very tasty dish, a combination of interesting flavours and textures which has proved very popular with all who have tasted it.

The Avocado Melon Salad (p.63) complements the casserole very nicely, although it is more seasonal in terms of availability, whereas the casserole can be enjoyed at any time of year and is essentially a meal in itself.

May be microwaved, but oven baked is recommended. Freezes well.

3 tbsp oil
1 medium onion, peeled and chopped finely
4 cloves garlic, crushed
2 stalks celery, chopped small
400g pumpkin, peeled and chopped into small cubes
150g cauliflower, broken or cut into small florets
1 cup raw peanuts, chopped roughly
2 bananas, peeled and cut into 2.5cm chunks
¾ cup red lentils
2 tsp red or hatcho miso (or yeast extract such as Marmite) — mix to a paste with a little water
1½ cups water
1 tsp lemon zest (grated rind)
3 tbsp lemon juice
2 tsp good quality curry powder
1 tsp garam masala powder
¼ tsp nutmeg
1 tsp green herb instant stock powder
1 tbsp fresh oregano, finely chopped or 1 tsp dried
2 tsp honey
1½ tsp freshly ground black pepper
3-4 small dried red chillies, crushed
2 tsp tomato paste
½ tsp salt or to taste
1½-1¾ cups tinned coconut cream (allow 1 410g tin)

Pre-heat the oven to 190°C.

Heat the oil in a large pan over a medium-low heat. Saute the onion, garlic and celery in the oil until the onion softens. Stir in the pumpkin, cauliflower, peanuts and bananas, cook for 2-3 minutes, stirring.

Add all the remaining ingredients, but only 1 cup of the coconut cream. Mix thoroughly, then pour into a 1.5-litre casserole dish with a lid.

Cover and bake at 190°C for approximately 40 minutes. Stir in the remaining ½-¾ cup coconut cream and cook for 10 minutes more.

Avocado Melon Salad

½ rock melon, peeled and diced
2 zucchini
¾ cup sprouted brown lentils or alfalfa sprouts
1 orange, peeled and diced (catch any juice and add)
juice of ½ lemon
1 ripe avocado, peeled and diced
vinaigrette dressing

This recipe is included here because it complements the Burmese Nut Casserole so well. It is possible, though, to make this salad into a light meal for 4 — see additions below.

   Place the prepared rock melon in a serving bowl.
Chop the zucchini into small dice, and add with the sprouts and orange.
Sprinkle the avocado with the lemon juice and add. Sprinkle with vinaigrette and toss gently.

Additions
For a main course salad, your choice of some or all of these (plus anything else you fancy) to produce a zesty, taste-packed light meal:

1 extra orange, peeled and diced
1 cup wholemeal croutons*
2 hard-boiled eggs, chopped
2 tomatoes, segmented
100g cheese, diced — cheddar, fetta, or gruyere, or a mix, depending on what taste you want or ½ cup cottage cheese
12 green olives
1 capsicum, seeded and sliced into thin strips
2 stalks celery, sliced thinly on a diagonal
½ cup toasted sunflower kernels or pumpkin kernels or toasted nuts such as peanuts, walnuts etc.**

Croutons can be made in a microwave. Simply butter both sides of 2 medium wholemeal bread slices, cut to crouton size, then place in single layer on a platter and microwave on high for 3 minutes.

**Kernels and nuts can be toasted in a microwave — either dry roast without any oil, or add 1 tsp oil per cup measure, then microwave on high, uncovered, 4 minutes for kernels and sesame seeds, or 5 minutes for nuts, stirring twice during the cooking time.*

This dish is ideal for busy people, as it is really a one-dish meal, satisfying without being heavy, and very tasty. (Most children enjoy noodle dishes, and this one is no exception — you may, however, wish to omit the chillies.) Essentially, bami goreng is a noodle stir fry, so, as with all such dishes, you should prepare the individual ingredients first. If you wish, you could add cooked vegetables such as lightly steamed or microwaved zucchini or corn on the cob, and/or a simple green salad garnished with persimmon slices, if they are available.

* You could replace these noodles with ordinary vermicelli or even spaghetti noodles if necessary.

** and *** Oyster sauce and fish sauce are available from larger supermarkets or Asian specialty stores. Since each has its own distinctive flavour it is preferable to use them when stated. Otherwise simply add more light soya sauce to your taste.

Bami Goreng

454g packet of thin round chinese noodles, egg or plain*
3 tbsp oil
1 large onion, peeled and chopped finely
2 tsp finely chopped root ginger
2-3 cloves garlic, crushed
3 small dried red chillies, very finely chopped (optional)
1 medium-sized carrot, cut into thin julienne sticks
3 cups broccoli florets, sliced thinly
1 cup celery, sliced thinly on the diagonal
^{1}/3 cup stock or water
¼ cup (4 tbsp) light soya sauce
1 tbsp oyster sauce**
1 tbsp fish sauce***
lots of freshly ground black pepper
^{1}/3 cup pine nuts, almonds, cashews or walnuts
thin slices of persimmon for garnish if available

Cook the noodles in boiling water until just tender, according to instructions. Drain and toss in 1 tsp oil to keep them from sticking together.

Heat the oil in a wok, preferably, or a large heavy-bottomed frypan.

Saute the onion, ginger, garlic and chillies over a low-medium heat until the onion softens. Add the prepared carrot and saute for 1 minute, then add the broccoli and celery. Saute for 3 more minutes, approximately, then stir in the remaining ingredients, including the nuts.

Now add the cooked and drained noodles, tossing with 2 forks or serving spoons if you wish, to separate the noodles and combine with the other ingredients and the sauce.

Ensure that the noodles are heated through and piping hot, then serve immediately, garnished with thin slices of persimmon if available.

Pakistani Vegetable Curry

600g potatoes
300g cauliflorets
2 tbsp (30g) margarine or butter
1 small onion, peeled and sliced thinly
2 tsp fresh ginger, peeled and very finely chopped
1½ tsp turmeric
1 tsp salt
½ tsp chilli powder
1 tsp garam masala
2 tbsp toasted sunflower kernels for garnish*
finely chopped parsley

Peel the potatoes and cut into very small dice.
Slice the cauliflorets into thin slices (keep some of the stalk with the flower).
Melt the margarine or butter in a deep frypan with a lid, and saute the onion and ginger over a gentle heat until the onion softens. Add the turmeric, salt and chilli powder and stir in. Place the prepared potatoes, then the cauliflower in the pan and mix gently. Cover the pan tightly and cook over a medium-low heat for 20-30 minutes, or until the potato is tender. Check that the bottom is not sticking and stir occasionally. If the bottom is sticking, turn down the heat a little.
Lastly, stir in the garam masala carefully, to avoid breaking up the potato, and cook uncovered for 5 more minutes. This dish should cook beautifully without any added water; the result should be a moist dish, but without any sauce surrounding the vegetables.
Garnish with the toasted sunflower kernels and sprinkle with the chopped parsley.

This is a 'dry' curry with a wonderful flavour, but it also combines well with any other curry dishes. If serving it as the sole main dish, accompany it with salads, plus a choice of other staples if you wish such as a dhal (p.66), chapatis or puris (p.67) and/or rice. Add some sambals and raitas (see p.100).

Instead of making chapatis or puris (p.67), try the commercially packaged poppodoms (papads). These are a very thin pancake-shaped delicacy, available from large supermarkets, delicatessens or specialty stores. Normally they are shallow fried in oil for a few seconds on either side, whereupon they transmute into puffy and crisp morsels, delicious to eat with curries. If using a microwave, however, you need no oil to achieve very similar results — simply place 2 poppodoms at a time on a paper towel and cook, uncovered, on high power for 45 seconds.

*The easiest way to toast the sunflower kernels is to microwave on high, uncovered, for 4 minutes — stir twice.

This dish may be reheated by microwave and can be frozen.

Lentil Dhal

Dhal is a common food in India, and may be made from several different pulses — mung beans, split peas, lentils, etc. They are high in vitamins and, when served with rice (especially brown) or chapatis, have a good quality protein content. (Pulses and grains, when served together, complement each other to provide a complete protein.) Apart from all this, a dhal tastes good and can be served with any curried food, or on its own with chapatis, dosas (p.67) or rice, yoghurt and salads. Dhals are simple to make, and cost very little, too.

lentils

1 cup red lentils
3 tbsp margarine or ghee
1 large onion, peeled and chopped finely
3 garlic cloves, crushed
2 tsp ground coriander
1 tsp ground cumin
1 tsp turmeric
½ tsp chilli powder
1 tsp salt
1 tsp freshly ground black pepper
1½ tbsp lemon juice
3 cups water

Wash the lentils and drain thoroughly.
Melt the margarine or ghee in a heavy-bottomed saucepan, add the onion and garlic and saute over a gentle heat until the onion is soft.
Add all the spices and seasonings and saute for 1-2 minutes.
Now add the washed and drained lentils, the lemon juice and the water.
Bring to the boil, then lower the heat and simmer, uncovered, for 15-20 minutes. Stir regularly and add extra water if necessary.

Potato Dosas (or Chapatis or Puris)

1 cup cold mashed potatoes
1 cup wholemeal flour
2 tbsp oil
2 tbsp warm water
¾ tsp salt
freshly ground black pepper

Mix the potatoes into the flour with your fingertips. Sir in the oil, water and seasonings with a knife until it 'balls', then turn onto a lightly floured board. Knead 6-10 times.
Divide into 6-8, form each portion into a ball, then roll as thinly as possible into a circle shape. To make them absolutely circular, place a small bread and butter plate over the circle and cut around this with a knife.
Cook for a few minutes on either side in a dry heavy-bottomed frypan over a medium-high heat. Press down and flip over at intervals until both sides are crisped and speckled dark brown.
Serve them with a vegetable curry and/or dhal, plus some plain yoghurt and chutneys. Add a salad if you wish.

To make chapatis, use the recipe for dosas, but substitute plain flour for the potatoes, and increase the amount of (warm) water for mixing to approximately ¾ cup. Increase the kneading time to 4-5 minutes, but apart from these changes, the procedure and cooking is the same as for dosas.

To make puris, the recipe and procedure is exactly the same as that outlined for chapatis, except that the puris are deep fried in oil for about 30 seconds on each side, then drained on kitchen towels. With puris, the oil content should be taken into consideration, although they taste so good. You could make half of the recipe mixture into chapatis, then add some oil to your pan and make the other half of the mixture into puris if you want to cut down on the oil content but find the lure of crisp, flaky, tender puris impossible to resist.

Dosas are very similar to chapatis, but have a higher nutritional value as they contain potatoes, rather than just flour. They may be served instead of chapatis or puris as part of a curry meal, or for a very simple meal, they complement Lentil Dhal (p.66) very nicely indeed. Add a salad and you have a tasty, nutritious and filling meal.
In curry-eating countries a great variety of breads are served, usually instead of rice, and most are of the flat, unleavened variety. The chapati is probably the best known throughout the Western world; roti is simply a thicker version of a chapati. A paratha is similar, but the dough is brushed with melted butter before cooking and they are often served stuffed. Puris are deep fried, puffed and light.*

The unleavened breads of curry-eating countries are torn and wrapped around the curried food, using the fingers. Rice may also be served, however.

This mixture may be doubled and the uncooked breads may be frozen, placing each between sheets of cling wrap or dividers.

Not recommended for microwaving.

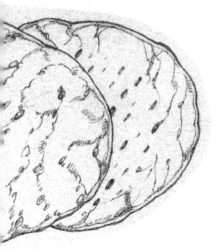

These red lentil 'cakes' or patties are very simple and quick to make, and make a tasty accompaniment to any curry meal, served with yoghurt to garnish. They can also form the basis of a light meal if served with a sate sauce, brown rice or noodles and a crunchy salad.

The lentils for these cakes do need to be soaked before cooking, which requires just a thought before you race off for the day. Set the lentils to soak in the morning, or for 6 hours before the evening meal. Makes about 14 medium-sized patties.

Not recommended for cooking in a microwave; may be frozen, then reheated in a hot oven or microwave.

This sauce is very quick to make, and can be served as a sauce for the red lentil cakes, or you could make a quick vegetable stir fry to accompany the lentil cakes. Simply saute 6 cups thinly sliced vegetables such as cauliflorets, broccoli florets, mushrooms, celery sliced on a diagonal, beans etc. in 2 tbsp oil for 3-4 minutes. Stir in the sate sauce (there should be about ½ cup), then ¹/3 cup tinned coconut cream. Reheat and cook, stirring for 2 minutes more and serve immediately.

This sauce may be microwaved or frozen, and the quantity is very easily doubled.

Red Lentil Cakes with Sate Sauce

1 cup red lentils
1 tsp skinned and finely minced fresh ginger
2 garlic cloves, peeled
½ tsp chilli powder
1 tsp ground coriander
1 tsp salt
1 tbsp lemon juice
1 medium carrot, chopped
½ medium onion, chopped
freshly ground black pepper
½ cup water (reserved from soaking the lentils)
¼ cup oil

Wash the lentils and soak for 6-10 hours.
Drain the lentils while you prepare the rest of the ingredients, reserving ½ cup of the soaking water.
Place the lentils with all the remaining ingredients except the oil into a food processor and blend until they form a thick puree.
Heat the oil in a heavy-bottomed frypan, then drop in spoonfuls of the lentil mixture. Fry on each side for a few minutes, or until they are puffed up and golden brown. Add a little more oil if necessary.
Drain on paper towels. Serve garnished with parsley and the sate sauce.

Sate Sauce

2 tbsp crunchy peanut butter
1-2 cloves garlic, crushed
2 tbsp light soya sauce
2 tbsp honey
¼-½ tsp chilli powder
¼ tsp salt
1 tsp lemon juice
½ cup water
¹/3 cup coconut cream (optional)

Whisk all ingredients together in a small saucepan until combined. Simmer over a gentle heat for about 10 minutes, until the sauce is lightly thickened.
If you feel you'd prefer a milder flavoured sauce, mix in ¹/3 cup coconut cream and cook a few minutes longer.

Eggplant Siciliana

500g eggplant — 1 large or 2 small approx.
¼ cup oil
1 large onion, peeled and chopped
2 cloves garlic, crushed
½ cup red lentils
3 stalks celery, sliced
2 red capsicums, seeded and diced (green may be used)
425g tin peeled chopped tomatoes, plus juice or equivalent fresh
1 tbsp malt vinegar
1 tbsp sugar
1 cup stock or water
1 tsp salt
lots of freshly ground black pepper
2 tsp lightly chopped, drained capers
12 black olives, stoned and chopped approx. into quarters

Weigh and dice the unpeeled eggplant.

Heat the oil in a large pan over a gentle heat, then saute the onion and garlic until the onion softens.

Add the red lentils and cook, stirring, for 2-3 minutes, then add the celery and capsicums. Saute these for 4 minutes, then add the eggplant and saute for another 4 minutes approximately.

Now stir in the chopped peeled tomatoes, the tomato paste, vinegar, sugar, water, salt and pepper.

Next add the chopped olives and the capers and combine well.

Simmer over a gentle to moderate heat for about 15 minutes or until most of the liquid has evaporated.

Serve warm, at room temperature, or immediately, accompanied by steamed rice.

This speedy dish has its origins in Sicily, as is indicated by the inclusion of black olives and capers. It is cooked very like a ratatouille (traditional French vegetable stew), and both the olives and capers can be omitted if you really must, so perhaps it is truer to say that this is a significantly cosmopolitan dish. The inclusion of red lentils transforms it into a one-dish meal if served accompanied by steamed brown, white or glutinous rice plus a salad or two. Serve this dish hot if you wish, though it is even better served at room temperature or lightly warmed through.

There is no need to salt the eggplant. Do use red capsicums if possible, as their flavour is particularly appealing in this dish, and also because they retain their beautiful red colour throughout the cooking so that the dish looks most attractive when served.

Not recommended for microwaving, but may be frozen.

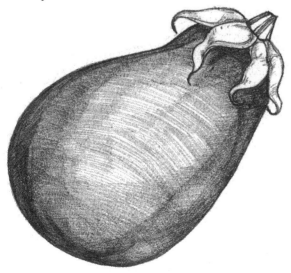

gnocchi

Gnocchi with Pine Nuts and Herbs

These gnocchi are delicious. Italian in origin, they are in fact little croquettes and can traditionally be made from potatoes, semolina or cornmeal — or from spinach and ricotta cheese. Cottage cheese, pine nuts and silver beet (or spinach) are used here, for convenience and nutrition; the inclusion of herbs, including mint, adds interest and a touch of 'zing'.

Not recommended for microwave cooking; may be frozen.

This recipe makes about 25 small balls, enough for 4-6 depending on what you serve them with. Pasta is obvious, and there is a wide range of shapes to choose from these days — vegeroni would be fine, spirals, shells, or fettucine. A mixture of plain and wholemeal pasta is delicious with this dish. Use 300-500g, depending on how many people you are serving.

*Pine nuts are best, but you could substitute walnuts.

350g silver beet or spinach leaves, thick stalk removed
2 tbsp fresh chopped basil leaves or 1½ tsp dried
1 tbsp fresh chopped mint leaves or 1 tsp thick mint sauce (not concentrate)
⅓ cup pine nuts*
2-3 cloves peeled garlic
1 cup cottage cheese (250g)
1 tsp salt
freshly ground black pepper
½ cup grated mozzarella or tasty cheddar cheese
⅔ cup wholemeal flour
2 eggs, lightly beaten with a fork

2 tsp margarine
½ cup fresh grated parmesan or tasty cheddar

Rinse silver beet or spinach leaves and shake dry. Place in a bowl and cover with cling wrap, then microwave on high for 4 minutes or place in a saucepan with no extra water, cover, and cook over a medium heat for 7 minutes, shaking occasionally to prevent sticking. Turn out to drain and cool in a sieve while you prepare the remaining ingredients. Chop the basil, mint, pine nuts and garlic together in a food processor, then place in a bowl. Chop the cooked silver beet finely, and squeeze out any excess liquid firmly with your hands. Add to the bowl with the nuts and herbs, then add the remaining ingredients and combine well.

Place a very large saucepan of lightly salted water on the stove and bring to the boil while you finish preparation of the gnocchi.

Using floured hands, roll the mixture into balls about the size of a walnut (in its shell) and place on a large plate, ready to cook. (Don't pile them on top of each other as they may stick together.)

When the water is boiling, drop in about half the gnocchi, depending on the size of the saucepan. They shouldn't be crowded for space, as they will at first sink to the bottom but later rise to the top of the water. Cover and simmer for 10 minutes, then lift the balls from the water with a slotted spoon and allow to drain on kitchen paper. Repeat the process with the remaining gnocchi.

Place the gnocchi in a single layer on a buttered, ovenproof plate. Dot each gnocchi with a smidgen of margarine or melt 2 tsp butter or margarine and pour over. Now sprinkle ½ packed cup of grated parmesan (or cheddar) over the top of the gnocchi. They may be left at this stage, until 10 minutes before serving.

Pre-heat a grill, then place the prepared gnocchi under it (about 15 cm from the grill itself) and cook for approximately 8-10 minutes, until the cheese is melted and the gnocchi are heated through.

A tomato sauce smothers the flavour of these gnocchi; a more delicate sauce is needed if you are serving them with pasta. Try heating ½ cup low fat cream, or ⅔ cream and ⅓ plain yoghurt with some seasoning if you wish, just before the pasta is cooked. Stir 2-3 tbsp toasted sesame seeds into the cream just before serving, plus ¼ tsp sesame oil (optional), then pour over the pasta. Serve the gnocchi separately on a presentation platter garnished with tomato wedges and parsley. Add a green salad, plus cooked vegetables of your choice, and some crisp wholemeal bread sticks if you wish.

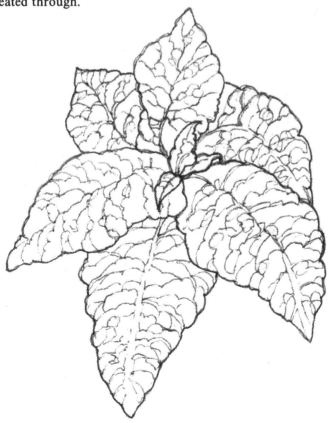

Creamy Herbed Pasta

This dish is popular with everyone, and so easy to prepare. Try serving it with a light dish such as Eggplant Siciliana (p.69) — it is also an ideal pasta dish to follow an antipasto (p.80), accompanied by a green salad and some heated crusty wholemeal breadsticks. Try it using a mixture of plain and wholemeal pasta, or vegeroni for a change. Although cream is used here, it is low fat (light) cream, and remember that this amount of pasta should satisfy at least 4 and possibly 6 adults, depending on what is served with it. The amount of saturated fat likely to be consumed by each individual is relatively small.

Long life low fat or light cream is ideal for this dish, especially as it can be kept in the pantry so you can produce this pasta at a moment's notice.

400g pasta, preferably a mixture of plain and wholemeal
2/3 cup low fat or light cream
1 tsp margarine
2 tbsp finely chopped parsley
2 tbsp finely chopped chives
2 tsp fresh oregano or ¾ tsp dried
2-4 cloves garlic, crushed
½-¾ tsp salt
freshly ground pepper
2 tsp margarine
½ cup toasted pumpkin kernels*
grated parmesan

Cook the pasta in lots of boiling salted water until just tender, then drain thoroughly.
While the pasta is cooking, heat the cream and the 1 tsp margarine in a small saucepan over a very gentle heat. Add the parsley, chives, oregano and garlic, then stir in the seasonings. Bring the sauce just to the boil, then remove from the heat.
Add the 2 tsp margarine to the cooked pasta and stir in. Now transfer the pasta to a heated serving dish, pour the cream and herb mixture over it, then toss lightly to mix. Sprinkle the toasted pumpkin kernels over the top of the pasta and serve immediately.
Grated parmesan may by passed around at the table as an accompaniment if you wish.**

*The easiest way to toast the pumpkin kernels is to toast them uncovered, on high, in a microwave for 3-4 minutes, stirring every minute or toast them in a heavy-bottomed pan over a gentle heat, stirring constantly.

**If no parmesan is available, grated Swiss or even tasty cheddar can be substituted.

Pesto for Pasta

¼ cup pine nuts*
200g spinach or silver beet leaves weighed with central stem removed
¼ cup olive oil
5 cloves garlic, crushed
1 cup parsley, thick stems removed
1½ tbsp dried basil (½-²/3 cup fresh chopped)
1 425g tin whole tomatoes, drained or equivalent fresh chopped
½ tsp salt or to taste
lots of freshly ground black pepper
1 440g tin tomato puree
½ cup grated parmesan cheese**

   Place the pine nuts in a processor and blend until finely chopped.
Wash and shake the excess water off the spinach/beet leaves. Chop the leaves roughly, then add to the nuts in the processor in 3 lots, along with the olive oil. Combine well.
Add the garlic, parsley and basil, then the drained tomatoes and pepper. Blend.
Place the tomato/basil mixture into a medium-sized saucepan, add the tomato puree and grated cheese. Stir to combine.
Simmer over a gentle heat for 4-5 minutes, then serve.

Pesto has long been recognised as one of the most delicious sauces to serve with pasta, but one drawback is that to make it traditionally you must have fresh basil — and as basil is an annual, this can make life difficult for pesto lovers. Americans in recent years have, however, discovered that a very passable pesto can be made using dried basil, in combination with fresh parsley and spinach or silver beet leaves.
The ingredients for this 'winter pesto' don't vary greatly although the proportions do. My variation uses less olive oil, for example. The wonderful thing about this sauce is that it not only tastes great, but is so simple and quick to prepare.
You will need about 500g pasta to serve 4-6 people. Use any pasta you like, though fettucine or tagliatelle is probably most traditional. Pasta needs only a green salad and crusty french bread as accompaniments — ideal for a quick, casual meal for guests.

cheese

parsley

Not recommended for microwave cooking or freezing.

Walnuts can be substituted for the pine nuts.

**Tasty cheddar can be substituted for the parmesan if necessary.*

Seafood

groper

Pan-Fried Fish with Orange Gingered Sauce or Red Capsicum Sauce

Prepare one of these elegant sauces to accompany fish fillets, and you can have a sophisticated meal prepared in no time at all. The sauces can, of course, be served with poached or microwaved fillets, depending on what fish you are serving — groper, tarakihi or snapper, for example. A personal recommendation, though, is to serve either of these sauces with pan-fried groper steaks or fillets.

6 groper steaks (3 if really large, you can halve them) or fillets for 6 people
plain flour with a little salt and freshly ground black pepper
45 g margarine or butter

Toss the fish steaks or fillets in the flour, then shake off any excess.
Heat the butter in a large, heavy-based frypan over a medium heat.
Add the fish in 1 layer, then cook for 3-4 minutes (depending on the thickness of the fish) on each side, until the flesh is white through to the middle when prised gently apart with a knife.
Arrange on a heated serving plate and pour over the sauce of your choice, accompanied by garnishings.

Orange Gingered Sauce

This sauce is best made within 3 hours of serving, as the orange rind can impart a slightly bitter taste if left longer.
Try serving fish and this sauce with lightly steamed broccoli or courgettes, plus baked potatoes and a green salad.

rind of ¾ of 1 medium orange
1 tbsp margarine or butter (15g)
1 tsp peeled and very finely chopped fresh ginger
½ cup orange juice (about 1½ oranges)
freshly ground black pepper
2-3 tsp honey
1 tsp cornflour
2 tsp water
1 kiwifruit, peeled and chopped or cut into rings

Peel the rind from ¾ of 1 orange using a potato peeler. Try to peel lightly, so that you avoid peeling any pith with the rind. Cut the rind into very thin, long strips.
Melt the margarine or butter in a small saucepan over a gentle heat.
Add the ginger and saute for 1-2 minutes.
Pour in the orange juice and stir in the prepared rind.
Add a few grinds of black pepper and the honey. Mix the cornflour and water to a paste and add when the sauce is almost at simmer point, stirring.
Bring just to the boil then pour over the fish. Garnish with the kiwifruit and serve.

Red Capsicum Sauce

2 tbsp margarine or butter (30g)
2 cloves garlic
1-2 red capsicums, seeded and diced — 1 cup of diced flesh
½ cup water
2 tsp lemon juice
1 tsp sugar
¾ tsp salt
freshly ground black pepper
1½ tsp cornflour mixed with 2 tsp water
sprig of fresh dill leaves to garnish

Melt the margarine or butter in a small saucepan, then saute the garlic for 1 minute over a gentle heat.
Add the diced capsicum and saute for another 2 minutes. Pour in the water and lemon juice with the sugar and seasonings. Bring just to the boil, then stir in the cornflour paste and reheat.
Serve poured over the cooked fish, garnished with a sprig of dill.

This is another sauce which should be served soon after preparation for best results. Try serving fish with this sauce accompanied by pasta into which a little warmed cream, finely chopped herbs and seasoning have been stirred. Add to this lightly steamed broccoli and a green salad.

The red capsicums used for this sauce not only give it a unique flavour (don't use green capsicums), but a wonderful colour. A feathery sprig of fresh dill is a perfect garnish if you have it.

groper

Fresh Mussel, Leek and Tarragon Quiche

For something just a bit different and special, try a light, creamy mussel quiche delicately flavoured with fresh tarragon. Fresh greenshell mussels are used, though it could be adapted for the smaller blue variety. Once the mussels are removed from the shell (either raw or lightly poached),* they can be left, covered, in a refrigerator for up to 8 hours — until you are ready to cook the quiche. If you are preparing ahead, shell the mussels, saute the leeks and make the pastry.

*To remove a raw mussel from its shell, slide a small sharp knife between the shell halves and around the inside of the shell (mussels usually attach to just one side of the shell).
To poach the mussels, scrub the shells and remove the beards by pulling gently.
Place 1 cup water in a large pan, add the mussels in their shells, then cover and cook for 3-5 minutes. Lift from the pan as soon as the shells open.

Pastry Crust

To line a 23cm quiche or flan tin, preferably with a removable base. This is a favourite all purpose short crust pastry.

½ cup wholemeal flour
½ cup plain flour
¼ cup grated cheddar cheese
50g cold margarine or butter
¼ cup very cold (preferably iced) water

Place the flours and cheese in the bowl of a food processor bowl.
Dice the margarine or butter and place on top of the other ingredients.
Process using the pulse control, adding the water slowly as you do so. (You may not need to use quite the full amount of water.) When the mixture starts to 'ball', press the moistened crumbs together with your fingers and place in a plastic bag or wrap. Refrigerate for at least 30 minutes if time permits.
Roll out on a lightly floured board to fit the buttered quiche tin.
If you wanted to make this quiche a little more sophisticated, line the quiche tin with layers of filo pastry. Brush every second layer with melted butter, then lay the pastry into the tin. Trim the edges to fit the tin.

Filling

500-750g fresh mussels in shell (15-20 greenshell mussels), which should produce about 1¹/₃ cups of chopped mussels when shelled or same quantity of lightly poached, shelled mussels
1½ cups thinly sliced leeks
1 tbsp (15g) margarine or butter
4 medium size eggs, or 3 large
1 tbsp finely chopped fresh tarragon or 1 tsp dried
½ cup sour cream
½ cup milk
½ tsp salt
lots of freshly ground black pepper
¾ cup grated Swiss or gruyere cheese (or tasty cheddar will do)

Pre-heat the oven to 200°C.
Chop each mussel into 3-4 pieces.
Saute the leeks in the margarine or butter over a medium-low heat until they soften.
Lay the leeks evenly in the bottom of the quiche, then top with the chopped mussels.
Beat the eggs with the tarragon, sour cream, milk and seasonings, then mix in the cheese. Pour over the leeks and mussels and bake immediately at 200°C for 30-35 minutes or until the filling is set. You may have to turn the oven down to 180°C after 20 minutes if the quiche appears to be cooking too quickly.

Don't discount frozen mussels for use in this recipe if you want to produce it without having to run out and purchase fresh ones. Frozen, shelled mussels are available commercially. Very lightly steamed, then blast frozen, their taste and texture are excellent.
You can replace the mussels with 1 210g tin of salmon or tuna, drained and flaked.

This recipe is unsuitable for microwaving but may be frozen.

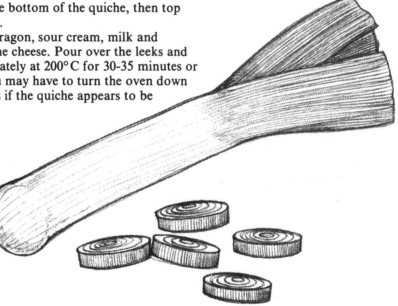

Commercially bought marinated mussels have become very popular over recent years, so much so that it's easy to overlook the fact that you can very quickly marinate fresh mussels yourself and produce a real taste treat for an entree or a salad meal.

These mussels could also be served as part of an antipasto dish, followed by a simple pasta meal such as Creamy Herbed Pasta (p.72) — wonderful! Other antipasto dishes you could include as a selection platter are Eggplant Siciliana (p.69) served at room temperature, olives, dill pickles or mixed pickles (p.112), sliced mushrooms marinated in a lemony vinaigrette for 3 hours or more and garnished with finely chopped parsley, melon and/or more avocado slices served with lemon wedges etc. (For a special occasion you could also add pieces of smoked salmon or Smoked Eel Pâté (p.105), cooked prawns or crayfish etc.)

Use the large greenshell variety of mussel for this recipe. They must be fresh, so the shells should be closed when you buy them. If they open before you use them, however, don't worry; if there is some response from the shell when you run cold water over them, or attempt to remove the beard, they are still fresh. It is more humane to use them as soon as possible, though.

Just a point of interest — mussels contain more iron than red meats!

Marinated Fresh Mussels

Scrub the mussels and remove the beard by pulling firmly. To remove them from their shells, slide a small sharp knife around the inside of the shell — they should just slip out. Marinated mussels should be ready to eat after 3 hours, although they can be left in their marinade, covered, for 2-3 days. For best results, though, marinade them for 4-12 hours. This recipe can easily be altered to accommodate a greater or smaller quantity of mussels.

800g-1kg large fresh mussels (about 24)
½ cup lemon juice
¾ tsp salt
lots of freshly ground black pepper
3 tbsp olive oil
3 garlic cloves, crushed
¾ tsp good quality mustard, such as Dijon
¾ tsp finely chopped fresh basil, oregano or tarragon

Place the shelled mussels in a shallow dish, in one layer. Whisk the remaining ingredients together in a bowl with a fork and pour over the mussels. Cover and refrigerate, turning occasionally.

basil

Fish, Apple and Herb Patties

500g boneless fish fillets (deep sea cod is very good, gurnard or lemonfish)
1 toast cut slice white or light wholemeal bread
1 medium onion, peeled and quartered
1 medium-sized Granny Smith apple, cored and quartered
¼ cup fresh parsley, roughly chopped
1 tbsp fresh basil, chopped, or oregano (or 1 tsp dried)
2 tbsp lemon juice
¼ cup milk
1 tsp salt
freshly ground black pepper
3 tbsp oil, more as needed

Chop the fish fillets into 1-2 cm pieces.
Crumb the bread in a food processor, then remove from the processor bowl and measure — this should yield ½ cup fresh breadcrumbs.
Place the onion, the unpeeled apple pieces, parsley, basil and lemon juice into the processor bowl and process until finely chopped.
Now add the breadcrumbs, milk, salt, pepper and the chopped fish. Process for about 20 seconds, until all the ingredients are chopped and well combined (don't overmix).
Heat the oil in a medium-large, heavy-based pan over a medium heat.
Take spoonfuls of the patty mixture and, using wholemeal flour, form into slightly flattened, medium-sized patties.
Fry 4-5 at a time, for about 3 minutes each side. Drain on kitchen paper, and keep the first ones hot in an oven while the remainder cook.

These simple patties are truly delicious, and quite different from usual fish patties. Children enjoy them as much as adults, and as they are moist and tender just as they are, there is no need for a sauce to serve with them. Try them served with Creamy Herbed Pasta (p.72), lightly steamed or microwaved broccoli and a green or tomato salad. (They're also delicious served with Curried Pumpkin Frittata, p.50.)

These patties tend to 'spit' a little when you cook them, because of the juice from the apple, so choose a pan which has a lid, and cover them partially as they cook if this does occur.

These patties freeze very well, and can be reheated from frozen in a microwave.

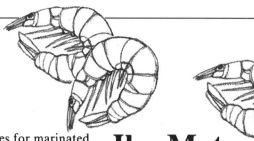

These recipes for marinated fish are not new. Ika Mata (marinated fish in coconut cream) is a great delicacy in the Pacific, where our family lived for 2½ years. The cream squeezed from fresh grated coconuts is used there, of course, but tinned coconut cream makes a very acceptable substitute. The Marinated Fish with Avocado Dressing is different, but just as delicious.

Use tarakihi, snapper, hoki or lemonfish for these recipes. If you haven't enough lemon juice to cover the fish you are marinating, up to ¼ of the quantity of lemon juice may be replaced by white vinegar.

You can include other seafood in either of these recipes. For a special occasion (such as Christmas Day) you could add cooked shrimps, prawns, crayfish or crab pieces to the drained marinated fish. Surimi is also available now; this is a hoki by-product and is usually crab flavoured, as in crab sticks. It is also sold as seafood salad at an affordable price, especially in view of the fact that a little goes a long way. It can be used in dishes such as these, in omelettes, rice dishes, in crepe fillings etc., as can any of the above mentioned.

Ika Mata

500g fresh white boneless fish, diced
lemon juice to cover
½ onion, sliced finely
1 cup tinned coconut cream (approx.)
chopped chives to garnish
1 small red capsicum, cut into dice or sliced into strips

Cover the diced fish with lemon juice and leave to marinate for 4-12 hours, covered, in the refrigerator. Stir occasionally. Pour off the lemon juice and drain the fish. Remove the onion slices if desired.
Place in an attractive serving bowl and pour over the coconut cream.
Garnish with a few chopped chives and the red capsicum strips or dice if available.

Marinated Fish with Avocado Dressing

500g fresh boneless white fish, diced
lemon juice to cover
½ onion, sliced finely

Cover the diced fish with lemon juice, then leave to marinate in the refrigerator, covered, for 4-12 hours. Stir occasionally. Pour off the lemon juice and drain. Remove the onion slices if desired.

Avocado Dressing

1 avocado, peeled and chopped and stone removed
2 tbsp lemon juice
1 tbsp olive oil
¼ tsp chopped fresh tarragon (optional)
2 tsp very finely chopped chives
½ cup lite sour cream
¼ cup plain yoghurt
½-¾ tsp salt
freshly ground black pepper

This dressing is best prepared shortly before it is to be served.

Place all the ingredients into the bowl of a food processor and process with the metal blade until smooth and creamy. Serve as soon as possible, in a separate dish so that people can help themselves to the amount they want.

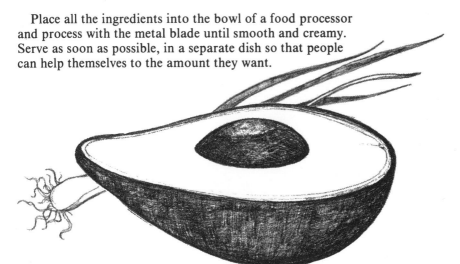

Ika Moana Nui a Kiva

Microwaved Ika

This is a superb dish served with a special sauce, one which can accompany the very best of fish. Orange roughy is my favourite, but you can use any firm, white-fleshed, boneless fillets. The fish is cooked very simply, and the sauce has a tropical bias, with fresh orange juice and coconut cream — reminiscent of my years in the Cook Islands, and especially of fish from the Aitutaki lagoon.

Try it served with baked potatoes, steamed or microwaved beans and a lettuce/vinaigrette salad, garnished with avocado slices, tomato wedges and nasturtium flowers.

Orange roughy is wonderful microwaved and it also freezes very well, maintaining its flavour and texture. This makes it an excellent fish to have on hand in the freezer for a special meal, as it is one of the more expensive fish. Fresh hoki microwaves very well; and fresh snapper or tarakihi are also excellent for this dish.

You'll need 1 kg of fish to serve 6 people (or 6 medium fillets).

800g-1 kg fresh fish fillets (hoki, snapper, tarakihi or orange roughy are excellent)
2 tsp margarine or butter
1 tsp fresh chopped basil or oregano (optional), not dried

Place the fillets on a shallow platter or dish, in a single layer. Dot with margarine and sprinkle over the herbs if using. You will probably have to use 2 large flat dishes, and cook them one after the other. Cover the dishes with cling wrap and cook on high for 3-4 minutes, depending on how much fish you have on each dish and the depth of fillets. You should be able to see when the fish is cooked through, but check by piercing the middle of a fillet with a knife. It should be completely white, and should flake easily.

Lift the cooked fillets from any cooking liquid with a fish slice and transfer to a warmed serving platter. Pour over the sauce and arrange the garnishes attractively. Serve immediately.

Moana Nui a Kiva Sauce

15g (1 tbsp) margarine or butter
2 cloves garlic, crushed
2 tsp skinned and very finely chopped fresh ginger
¼ cup plus 1 tbsp fresh orange juice
¼ cup stock or water
¼ tsp salt
freshly ground black pepper
1 tsp green peppercorns in brine, drained and crushed
1 cup tinned coconut cream

Garnish
thin slices of whole orange
¼ cup slivered almonds
2 tsp butter or margarine

This sauce seems to complement microwaved, steamed or poached fish beautifully, but my personal preference is for microwaved.

Melt the butter or margarine in a small saucepan. Saute the garlic and ginger gently, over a low heat until slightly golden (don't burn).
Pour in the orange juice and stock/water, and add the salt and pepper. Bring to the boil and simmer for 5 minutes.
Add the crushed peppercorns and the coconut cream, return to the boil, then simmer for 10-12 minutes. The sauce should be reduced and slightly thickened at this stage.
Pour over the cooked fish and garnish with the slivered almonds and orange slices.
To prepare the garnish:
Toast the almonds in the butter until golden brown, then drain on a kitchen towel.
Slice an orange in half, through its equator, then cut thin whole slices from each half. Make a cut in these slices once, to the centre, then twist. (Green grapes could be used instead of the orange twists if wished.)

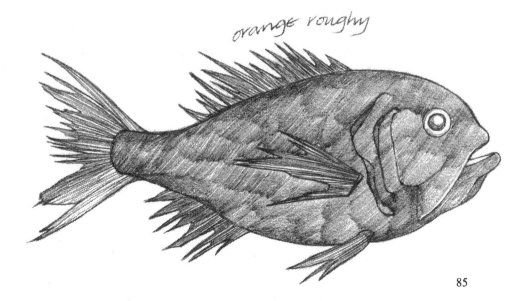

orange roughy

Coconut Crusted Fish with Phillip's Portofino Sauce

This wonderful sauce is a specialty of the Portofino Restaurant in Rarotonga, thanks to Phillip, the head chef. It is very simply made but a perfect accompaniment to fish, and can transform a simple dish into a gourmet delight.

For the purposes of this recipe, it doesn't really matter whether you microwave, poach, grill or pan fry the fish, or coat it with a coconut crust and fry.

Try serving this dish with fresh steamed asparagus, lightly cooked young carrot 'coins' and creamed potatoes (boiled, mashed and whipped with milk or lite sour cream).

Not suitable for microwaving or freezing.

Portofino Sauce

1 onion, peeled and finely chopped
2 cloves garlic, crushed
1 tbsp margarine or butter
1½ tsp good quality curry powder
2 ripe bananas, peeled and cut into 2.5cm chunks
1 cup tinned coconut cream
1½ tbsp lemon juice
½-¾ tsp salt (or to taste)
freshly ground black pepper

Heat the margarine or butter in a medium-sized saucepan, then saute the onion and garlic over a medium-low heat until the onion softens. Add the curry powder and cook for 2-3 minutes, stirring.
Add the chopped bananas and cook for 2-3 minutes more.
Now pour in the coconut cream and lemon juice and simmer for approximately 10 minutes, stirring regularly.
Pour over the cooked fish, garnished with some toasted coconut strands and toasted flaked almonds if desired.

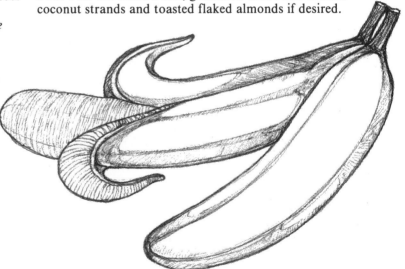

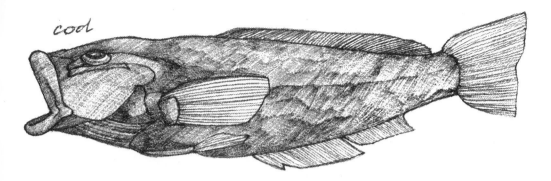

cod

Coconut Crusted Fish

6 suitably sized fish fillets or steaks — tarakihi, snapper, hoki, deep sea cod etc (about 1 kg)
plain flour
¼ tsp salt
freshly ground black pepper
¹/3 cup dry breadcrumbs
¹/3 cup desiccated coconut
¼ cup oil

Pat the fish dry with paper towels.
Toss the fish in the flour, then shake off the excess.
Beat the egg lightly with the milk and seasonings, then roll in
equal quantities of dry breadcrumbs and coconut — ¹/3 cup
of each should be enough.
Refrigerate the coated fillets for 30 minutes at this stage if
possible, to firm the coating.
Heat the oil in a large frypan over a medium heat.
Add the fish in a single layer, then cook for 3-4 minutes
(depending on the thickness of the fish) on each side, until
the flesh is white through to the middle and flakes easily
when prised gently apart with a knife.

Kiwifish Kebabs (with Kiwifruit and/or Peanut Sauce)

A kiwifruit sauce for fish? How about fish kebabs? Sounds interesting, doesn't it? But kiwifruit loses some of its colour and flavour during the cooking process, cream mellows the flavour too much, so finally — fresh orange juice, crushed green peppercorns, honey, a dash of mustard and a smidgen of sweet chilli sauce. And it takes only moments to prepare as there is no cooking involved!

These fish kebabs can be either barbecued or grilled; try serving them with a kiwifruit sauce, steamed rice and lots of salads — ideal for informal eating. Make half the quantity of each sauce if you'd like to provide a choice; a peanut (sate) sauce is very popular. Bluenose or groper are probably the best fish to use for kebabs, as the flesh is firm but doesn't dry out during grilling. Other fish you could use would be warehou (silver or deep sea), ling, gemfish or lemonfish.

Not suitable for freezing or microwaving.

750g white fish fillets
1 large or 2 small red capsicums
3 tbsp wine or cider vinegar or lemon juice
1½ tbsp water
5 medium kiwifruit — about 400g
2 tbsp orange juice
1 tsp green peppercorns, drained and mashed or capers
¼ tsp prepared mustard, preferably Dijon
3 tsp honey, runny or melted
⅛ tsp salt or to taste
freshly ground black pepper
dash of sweet chilli sauce (optional)

Dice the fish and the seeded capsicum into bite-sized pieces and place in a large shallow dish. Mix the vinegar or lemon juice and water together and pour over the fish/capsicum pieces. Allow to stand for 2 hours if possible, stirring occasionally. If you are preparing in advance, it may be kept, covered, in the refrigerator for 24 hours. If time is short, omit the marinating altogether and instead melt 2 tbsp margarine or butter and add 1 tbsp lemon juice for basting while the fish grills (basting is not necessary if the fish is marinated beforehand).

Now place the fish onto skewers ready for the barbecue or the grill, interspersing pieces of fish with the chopped capsicum (Kebab ingredients should not be pushed too tightly against each other on the skewers, as the more dense ingredients will then not cook in the middle so easily.)

Grill or barbecue the kebabs over a medium-high heat for about 3 minutes each side. Don't let them overcook and become dry — tend carefully at this stage, as they lose their translucency. Remove them to a heated serving plate and present as soon as you are satisfied that the kebabs are cooked right through.

Serve the sauce(s) separately, for guests to help themselves.

Kiwifruit Sauce

350-400g kiwifruit, peeled (5 medium kiwifruit)
2 tbsp fresh orange juice
1 tsp brine-packed green peppercorns, crushed
¼ tsp prepared mustard, such as Dijon
3 tsp honey, running or melted
⅛ tsp salt
freshly ground black pepper

Chop the peeled kiwifruit flesh into a food processor or
blender with all the remaining ingredients and blend to
combine well.
Pour into a serving bowl, cover and refrigerate if preparing
ahead — it will keep for 2 days or more if necessary — but
serve it at room temperature.
This sauce goes quite a long way as you don't need a lot of it
per serving.

Peanut (Sate) Sauce

½ cup crunchy peanut butter
½ tsp salt
1 tsp finely chopped or minced root ginger
1 tbsp fruit chutney or 2 tsp brown sugar
1½ tbsp lemon juice
2 tsp light soya sauce
½-1 tsp sambal oelek or 1 tsp sweet chilli sauce
1 cup water

*This peanut sauce is also
delicious served over any
steamed vegetable mixture.*

Place all the above ingredients into a small saucepan over
a gentle heat, stirring constantly.
Bring to the boil, then reduce heat and simmer for about 5
minutes, stirring, until smooth and thickened.

Spicy Fish Herb and Potato Bake

This easy recipe is a delight to serve to family or friends — the intriguing hint of sweet chilli, coupled with melt-in-the-mouth fish, garlic, herbs and potatoes make this an irresistable combination.

* Ensure that you buy the freshest, white-fleshed, boneless fillets possible: such as sole, brill, blue cod, lemon flake, hoki, etc.

4 large potatoes (800g), peeled
400g white fish fillets e.g. sole, blue cod, brill*
3 medium sized fresh tomatoes, sliced
2 large cloves garlic, crushed
$^1/_2$ cup finely chopped fresh majoram, oregano or basil leaves
salt and freshly ground pepper
$^1/_4$ cup water
2 tbsp Thai sweet chilli sauce
1 tbsp butter

Slice the peeled potatoes very thinly (or slice with the appropriate attachment for your food processor).
Either cook the potato slices in boiling water, uncovered, for about 4 minutes OR sprinkle with water, cover and microwave on high for 5 minutes.
Lightly grease an ovenproof dish, then arrange half of the par-cooked potato slices evenly across the bottom. Season with salt and pepper.
Layer the sliced tomatoes over the potatoes.
Now layer in the fish fillets, season and sprinkle with the crushed garlic, followed by the chopped fresh herbs then the remainder of the potato.
Mix together the water and the Thai sweet chilli sauce and pour over. Season and dot with the butter.
Cover tightly with foil or lid and bake at 180–190° C for 40–45 minutes.
Serves 4.

Szechuan Squid with Broccoli and Black Bean Sauce

Soak the black beans and prepare the vegetables before you start cooking. Then you can produce this dish in about 7-10 minutes.
Serve over plain steamed rice, white or brown, accompanied by a crisp green salad.

500g squid tubes (2-3 medium tubes)
2 tbsp black beans, soaked and mashed*
2 tbsp oil
1 medium-large onion, peeled and chopped
1 medium carrot, sliced into julienne sticks
3-4 cloves garlic, crushed
1 tsp finely chopped fresh ginger
2 stalks celery, sliced on a diagonal (about 200g)
1 capsicum, preferably red, seeded and sliced into strips
300g broccoli florets, sliced on a diagonal through stalks as well
1 cup stock or water
1 tbsp soya sauce
1 tsp chilli sauce
½-1 tsp salt
1 cup mung bean sprouts (optional)
1 tbsp cornflour mixed with 2 tbsp water

Cut the squid tubes so that they open out flat. Score the inner side with a small diamond pattern, taking care not to cut right through. This tenderises the squid and also encourages it to roll up attractively when it is stir fried. Now slice the squid into fine strips, about 1cm wide and 5-7cm long.
Soak the black beans with water to cover, for approximately 10 minutes. Then drain and mash with a fork.
Heat the oil in a wok, preferably, or a large heavy-based frypan. Saute the onion, garlic and ginger over a medium heat until the onion softens.
Add the prepared squid strips, stir fry for about 15 seconds, then add the celery, capsicum and broccoli. Stir fry to combine well, then add the stock or water, the mashed black beans, soya sauce, chilli sauce and salt. Stir fry for approximately 3-4 minutes, until the vegetables are just cooked but still crispy.
Stir in the bean sprouts if using, just to combine, then the cornflour mixed with water and cook very briefly until the sauce thickens. Check the seasoning and serve immediately.

Squid is perfectly suited to Asian cooking, as it is much more firmly textured than most other fish. It therefore retains its shape throughout the cooking process, even when cut into small pieces. In this simple dish, the squid is complemented perfectly by a black bean sauce.

Try to obtain squid tubes when you are cooking squid. These are the skinned and cleaned squid bodies, which require little or no preparation. Otherwise, you can buy whole squid, in which case you will have to remove the fine outer skin and clean them yourself. (Your fish retailer can tell you how to do this, it's not difficult.) Squid requires very little cooking — about 1 minute to be tender if cooking on a direct heat. This recipe is correct; although the cooking time is slightly longer it equals out because of the addition of the vegetables and the quantities involved.

Not suitable for microwaving or freezing.

**Black beans are fermented soya beans, readily available from Asian specialty stores and some supermarkets. They are inexpensive, nutritious and very tasty.*

This dish eventuated after an evening out with friends to a restaurant where the most popular entree served was squid rings. We enjoyed them so much ourselves that I couldn't resist experimenting at home with the flavour a few days later. Our friends have since sampled the results as a main course, and given it the 'thumbs up'. It may not be an exact recreation, but it tastes very similar, i.e. very good indeed, *and* it's simple and quick.

A wok is ideal for cooking this dish, although it is possible to use a large, heavy-bottomed pan. The quantities may be halved; the recipe as given will serve 4-6 as a main, depending on appetites and on what you serve with it. As a suggestion, serve it with a vegetable stir fry and steamed rice or noodles. It's also very nice served with Sushi and Coconut/Chilli Dipping Sauce (p.58).

Oyster sauce and hoi sin sauce are available at large supermarkets here and/or oriental commodity stores. Both sauces are commonly used in Chinese cooking (oyster sauce has an oyster extract base, and hoi sin has a soya bean base). Both are most useful flavourings to have on hand if you enjoy Chinese cuisine.

Not suitable for freezing or microwaving.

Spinach and Hoi Sin Squid

600-650 squid tube (3-4 medium sized)
3 tbsp oil
1 onion, peeled and finely chopped
2-3 cloves garlic, crushed
2-2¼ cups finely shredded spinach or silver beet leaves, well packed (100g approx.)
2 tbsp oyster sauce
3 tbsp hoi sin sauce
1 tsp light soya sauce
2 tbsp water

Slice the squid tube into 1cm wide rings.
Heat the oil in a wok or large heavy-based pan over a gentle heat. Saute the onion and garlic in the oil until the onion softens, then stir in the shredded spinach or beet leaves (central stalk removed). Saute for 1-2 minutes, until the spinach starts to cook down.
Turn the heat up to medium high.
Mix the oyster, hoi sin, soya sauce and water together.
Add the squid rings to the wok or pan and stir fry for a few seconds, then add the combined sauces and continue to stir fry.
It should be noted here that squid rings cook very quickly — depending on the temperature they are cooked at, and the quantity cooked, 30-40 seconds can be long enough. The variables are too great to be absolutely specific, but it's better to slightly undercook than overcook, though, as squid becomes quite rubbery if overcooked. It does have a much firmer texture than most fish, of course, but it should be tender and melt in the mouth.
This quantity of squid should be stir fried for about 3-4 minutes in a wok (less if you are cooking in a large frypan). The heat can't be too high or you will risk burning the sauce, which is quite thick, so tend carefully at this stage. If you are halving the quantities, it will cook more quickly. Squid is cooked as soon as it loses its translucent appearance and flaccidity. It turns opaque and firm but tender in texture. Serve immediately.

Baked Fish with Spiced Ginger and Yoghurt Sauce

800g fresh boneless fish fillets, e.g. ling
1 tsp salt
freshly ground black pepper to taste
2 tsp skinned and grated fresh ginger
1 clove garlic, crushed
¼ cup lemon juice
1¼ cups plain yoghurt (unsweetened)
2 tsp turmeric
1 tbsp garam masala
parsley sprigs to garnish (or fresh coriander)

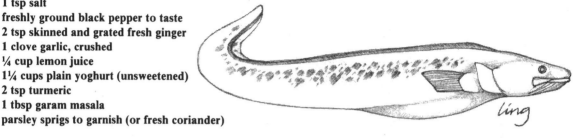

Place the fish fillets in a single layer in a shallow, ovenproof dish. If the fillets are thick, make one or two cuts in the thickest part on each side. If you are using ling, you may have to slice in half horizontally (through the depth of the fillets), as they can be quite thick.

Mix the salt and pepper, ginger, garlic and lemon juice, then pour this mixture over the fish and leave for 20 minutes, turning once or twice. Tip the dish to pour off the excess lemon juice (don't be too fanatical, and there is no need to discard the garlic and ginger). Mix the yoghurt, turmeric and garam masala and coat the fish with this. Leave for a further 20 minutes. Meanwhile, heat the oven to 200°C.

Place the yoghurt-coated fish, still in its ovenproof dish and in a single layer, into the oven. Bake, uncovered, for 10 minutes. Check at this stage, and you will find that the fish has shrunk to some extent as it has cooked, and that some cooking liquid has seeped into the yoghurt sauce. This can have the appearance of having 'curdled' slightly, but don't worry — it hasn't. Losing as little of the actual sauce as possible, carefully pour off the excess liquid. Baste with the sauce around the fish and return to the oven.

Bake for a further 10 minutes or until it is cooked. (Pierce the flesh with a knife and ease it apart a little to see that it is white right through.)

Transfer the fish to a heated serving platter, spoon the sauce over and garnish with chopped fresh parsley or coriander.

This recipe is Indian in origin, and as such has an authentic flavour, but is also simple to prepare. Serve it with rice, a sambal such as tomato and finely chopped onion; chutneys; roasted cashews or other nuts; a salad such as orange and celery with a vinaigrette dressing; and a dhal if you wish (p.66). This dish is *not* hot, so serve a chilli condiment with it if desired.

If you have time, try dividing your fish to make half quantities of both this dish and the Malay Fish Curry (p.94) for a superb Eastern meal.

Ling is ideal for this dish, also gemfish, blue warehou, hoki, hake or jack mackerel.

Malay Fish Curry

For curry lovers, this dish is a 'must' — quite irresistible. The idea was contributed by my friend Sue Carruthers, who is a restaurateur in Rarotonga, and after several trials I feel the results are as she intended. It makes a wonderful centrepiece for a curry meal, served with steamed long grain or glutinous rice, salads and sambals (side dishes such as chutneys), chapatis, toasted nuts and raitas (yoghurt-based side dishes such as cucumber or prunes in plain yoghurt — see p.100).

Firm-fleshed fish is preferable for this curry as you don't want it to break up. Ling is excellent in this respect, and it is my preference for this dish, although any of the fish specified are good. Ling doesn't absorb the curry flavour as much as the slightly more oily fish mentioned, but I prefer it for the taste/texture contrast it creates.

*Oyster sauce is an Asian sauce made from oysters and readily available in supermarkets or Asian specialty stores.

Not suitable for microwaving or freezing.

800-1 kg fresh fish fillets such as ling, jack mackerel, trevally, warehou, gemfish, monkfish or hake cut into 5 x 2cm cubes

Marinade
2 tbsp oil
2 tbsp thick mint sauce (not concentrate) or 1 tbsp finely chopped mint leaves
2 tbsp oyster sauce*
1 tsp light soya sauce
2 tsp good quality curry powder
juice and grated rind (zest) of 1 lemon
6 cloves crushed garlic
2 tsp skinned and grated fresh ginger

Combine all the marinade ingredients together in a non-metallic bowl and lay the fish in it. Mix gently, then cover the bowl and turn occasionally. Leave for 2 hours if possible.

soy sauce

ginger root

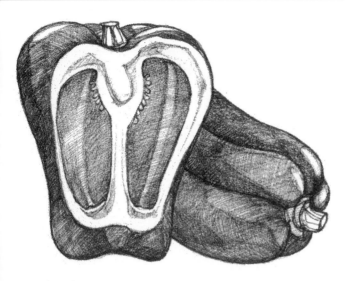

Sauce

2 tbsp oil or ghee
2 medium onions, peeled and halved then sliced thinly
1 capsicum, seeded and chopped or equivalent amount of celery
3 tsp coriander
2 tsp turmeric
1½ tsp chilli powder or at your discretion
2 tsp good quality curry powder
1 tsp freshly ground black pepper
2 cups water
1 tbsp malt vinegar
2 tbsp tomato paste
1½ cups tinned coconut cream
2 tsp garam masala
1 tsp salt
fresh chopped coriander or parsley for garnish

Heat the oil or ghee in a large heavy-based frypan or
saucepan.
Saute the onion and capsicum over a medium-low heat until
the onion softens.
Add the coriander, turmeric, chilli, curry and pepper and
saute for 5 minutes.
Add the water, vinegar, tomato paste and 1 cup of the
coconut cream. Cook uncovered, stirring occasionally, over
a gentle heat until the sauce is reduced and thickened —
about 30 minutes.
Now add the fish and the marinade to the sauce. Bring back
to the boil (just) and simmer very gently about 3-4 minutes.
Stir as little as possible, so as not to break up the fish.
Stir in the last ½ cup of coconut cream, the garam masala
and the salt and serve.
Garnish with fresh chopped coriander or parsley.

Pauatahanui Pasta

The Pauatahanui inlet is a special place to me, and this is one of my favourite recipes. The attractions of this dish are that it's very quick and easy to prepare, it tastes wonderful and, as with most pasta dishes, you need only a green salad and some crusty french bread to accompany it. Although this is a creamy sauce, it uses lite sour cream, which contains 40% less fat than ordinary sour cream or cream.

This recipe serves 4-6 adults, depending on appetites and on what you serve with it.

To appreciate this dish fully, I do recommend that you serve it with spinach (green) fettucine and it is worthwhile going to some trouble to find a red capsicum; both the flavour and the colour combination are superior in this dish, although a green capsicum may be substituted if red aren't available. Don't be alarmed if the sauce has too definite a taste before you pour it over the pasta — remember that there is a large quantity of pasta relative to the quantity of sauce, and so the sauce needs to be well flavoured to retain its individuality.

400-450g spinach fettucine
500g firm fish fillets
1 tbsp oil
1 tbsp margarine
1 medium onion, peeled and chopped finely
2-3 cloves garlic, crushed
1 medium-large red capsicum, seeded and diced
2 tsp lemon juice
¾ cup lite sour cream
9 flat anchovy fillets, drained and chopped finely
¾ tsp salt
freshly ground black pepper

Put the water on to boil for cooking the fettucine (remember the proportion is 4 litres of water to cook 500g pasta). Start the pasta cooking before you begin the Pauatahanui sauce, as it takes about the same time to cook as the fettucine (10 minutes).

Pat the fish dry using paper towels. Dice the fish into 1.25cm cubes.

Heat the oil and margarine together in a medium-large pan over a gentle heat.

fettucine

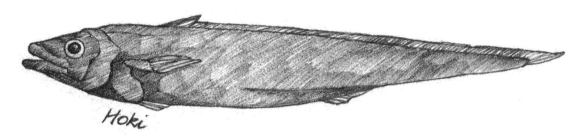

Hoki

Saute the onion and garlic together, adding the diced red capsicum just before the onion softens. Saute a little longer, then add the diced fish and saute carefully about 2 minutes. Mix the lite sour cream, lemon juice, anchovies and the salt and pepper together in a bowl with a fork, then pour into the pan with the fish. Add the optional oysters or shrimps etc. at this stage. Cook, stirring gently, to ensure that the fish doesn't break up at all, for about 3 minutes or until the fish is cooked through.

Drain the cooked pasta and transfer into a heated serving dish, then pour the sauce over this and serve immediately.

You may like to add $1/3$-$1/2$ cup cooked mussels, or cooked and deveined shrimps/prawns, or 6 raw oysters, chopped, when you add the cream and anchovies. This is an optional extra, however, and the dish tastes excellent as is. If you are making this addition, add the last anchovy (there are usually 10 in a 50g tin) with the 9 specified to keep the flavour balance.

Use hoki, warehou, gurnard (boned), mackerel, ling, bluenose or lemonfish; I've even used frozen hoki fillets for this dish, although fresh is always best, of course. If you are using frozen fish, remember to press it dry thoroughly with paper towels before using, to remove excess moisture. Don't thaw, just dice and cook for an extra minute.

Seafood in a tomato sauce is characteristically Italian, probably because tomatoes are so plentiful there. I've been suspicious of the combination in the past, feeling that the tomato flavour too often drowns the more delicate seafood taste. Mussels, however, have many good qualities, one of which is their ability to accommodate either a wine/garlic/cream sauce, or one that is tomato-flavoured. The sauce doesn't have to be totally non-assertive, either!

The mussels are cooked, still in their shell, in the sauce. This means that you don't have to pre-cook the mussels, and that you can quickly produce a meal which not only tastes great but looks stunning as well. Serve it with plain fettucine pasta (500g will feed 4-6), a simple green salad and some french bread, if you wish. If you're planning ahead, prepare the sauce then set aside before adding the mussels or cook the sauce to completion (including the addition of the mussels). When it cools sufficiently, remove the mussels from their shells and chop into 2-3 pieces each. Return them to the sauce, which may now be reheated.

A good quality Worcester sauce can do magical things for seafood. Add a touch of chilli if you like it.

Not suitable for freezing or microwaving.

Mussels Napoli

2 tbsp oil
1 onion, peeled and chopped
4 cloves garlic, crushed
1-2 small dried red chillies, chopped finely (optional)
1½ tbsp tomato paste
1 cup stock or water
1½ tbsp Worcester sauce
2 425g tins peeled tomato pieces or equivalent fresh
1 tsp sugar
¾-1 tsp salt
lots of freshly ground black pepper
18-20 greenshell mussels
¼ cup water
1 tbsp cornflour
3 tbsp finely chopped parsley
grated parmesan for passing at the table if desired

Heat the oil in a large deep saucepan or electric frypan with a lid.
Add the onion, garlic and chillies and saute over a gentle heat until the onion softens.
Stir in the tomato paste, stock or water, Worcester sauce and the undrained tomato pieces. You can crush the latter into smaller pieces if you wish, as the sauce cooks. Add the sugar, salt and pepper, and bring to the boil, stirring. Simmer gently, uncovered, for about 12 minutes. The sauce may be set aside at this stage if you are planning ahead.
Scrub the mussel shells and remove the beards — just pull them firmly and discard.
Just before you are ready to serve, place the mussels into the hot or reheated sauce, cover firmly and simmer gently for 5-6 minutes or until the shells are well open.
Mix the ¼ cup of water and the cornflour together and stir into the sauce. Bring back to the boil, stirring. Garnish with the chopped parsley and take to the table, along with heated serving plates.
Provide grated parmesan for an individual table garnish if you wish.

Recipes to Keep at Your Right Hand

Raitas

Raitas are yoghurt-based side dishes, served to accompany Eastern dishes, usually curries. They provide a palate-soothing contrast to the main dishes, and most are quite simply made. A plate of plain yoghurt is often served, but more often the yoghurt is used as a base and other ingredients are added to provide textural and flavour contrast. For example:
— pitted and chopped prunes
— seeded and sliced cucumber,
— sliced banana,
— chopped fresh peaches and orange segments,
— chopped fresh pears or plums.
Simply mix any of these options in the proportions you prefer, and serve.

Sambals

Sambals are also side dishes which commonly accompany curries, and are often chutneys, either fresh (such as chopped tomato and onion) or preserves. They can take almost any form, though, and can be savoury, sweet, pungent, salty or tart. Some very simple ones are:
— toasted nuts such as cashews, roasted peanuts and/or pumpkin kernels,
— pickled walnuts,
— onion rings, either finely sliced and served raw or browned in a little butter or oil,
— slices of fresh fruit,
— tomatoes, chopped and mixed with chopped onion, a little chilli, lemon juice and seasoning
— bananas, sliced and served plain or drizzled with lemon juice and dredged in coconut,
— cucumber, chopped and mixed with lemon juice and seasoning.

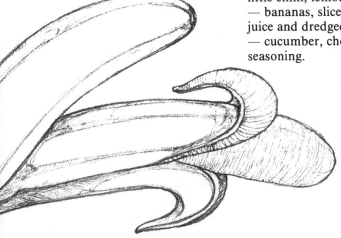

Creole Seasoning (for fish)

2 tbsp salt
3 tbsp paprika
3 tbsp garlic powder
2 tbsp dried oregano
2 tbsp dried basil
1 tbsp dried rosemary
1 tbsp black pepper
2 tbsp white pepper
2 tsp cayenne pepper
1 tbsp ground cumin or coriander

Mix all the ingredients together and store in an airtight container.

Simply brush fresh fish fillets on all sides with melted butter. Place some of the creole seasoning mix on a plate and coat the fillets with it.

Place fish in a lightly greased baking dish, well spaced, and bake in a hot oven at 200° C for approximately 10–15 minutes, depending on how thick the fillets are.

Note: For those who may find this seasoning a little too robust, try mixing 4–5 tbsp of the mix with ²/₃ cup dry breadcrumbs to coat 400g fish fillets.

Dip the fillets into a beaten egg, then toss in the breadcrumb/ creole mix and fry in a little oil until golden brown and cooked through.

It's very useful to have a seasoning which is entirely made of dry ingredients so that it can be made ahead of time, in bulk if you use a lot of it. It's *especially* useful when such a seasoning has a variety of uses.

This seasoning has quite a bite, so small children may find it too hot; but older children have been known to enjoy it sprinkled on oven-baked potato chips or skins, and even on popcorn.

Having this seasoning on hand ensures that you can produce a great fish dish in very little time and with virtually no effort. Team it with plain rice, or rice pilau; a fresh tomato salsa, perhaps, with fresh coriander; and some sauteed courgettes.

Use any fresh white fillets — lemon flake, blue cod or ling for example. Sole or even hoki are probably too thin. To complement the fish flavour and avoid overwhelming it, you should use this seasoning to coat thicker fillets.

Note: This recipe provides enough seasoning to coat fish for 2–3 meals for a family of 6, so you should have some extra to keep on hand.

Deep-fried — in a 'good health' cookbook? Well, yes — in moderate amounts, and on the odd occasion, why not? Unless a medically diagnosed condition indicates that fat intake should be stringently regulated, there should be no harm in the consumption of very moderate amounts of fats. Fat soluble vitamins such as A, D, E and K have nutritional value, and if fats are virtually excluded from the diet, the range of possible tastes and textures is severely limited. By all means, try to ensure that the fats you consume are polyunsaturated or, even better, monounsaturated.

Mussels cooked this way are just as good as oysters, in my view. Serve them simply with lemon wedges as an entree or try the Orange and Mint Dressing which is also good served with squid rings, or crab sticks.

Prepare the squid rings (cut the rings from squid tubes, in 4mm strips) and crab sticks in the same way as the mussels — flour, egg, then breadcrumb and deep fry for 1-2 minutes.

Open fresh live mussels with a sharp-bladed knife, and slip the mussels from the shells.
Remove the beards.
Coat the mussels with lightly seasoned flour, dip into beaten egg then dredge in dry breadcrumbs.
Deep fry in hot oil for 1-2 minutes, taking care not to overcook.

Deep-Fried Mussels, Squid Rings or Crab Sticks with Orange and Mint Yoghurt Dressing

Orange and Mint Dressing

This sauce is best made just before it is to be eaten, as the orange rind can develop a slightly bitter taste if left longer than 3–6 hours.

1/3 cup mayonnaise, preferably home-made*
1 tbsp fresh orange juice (generous)
1¼ tsp grated orange rind (zest)
½ tsp very finely chopped fresh mint leaves (measure) or thick mint sauce
freshly ground black pepper
½ tsp melted honey
½ cup plain yoghurt
1 tsp very finely chopped chives

Place all ingredients in a small bowl and whisk until well combined.

*Home-made Mayonnaise
1 egg
½ tsp salt
2 tbsp white or wine vinegar
1 cup oil

Place egg, salt and vinegar in a food processor bowl and combine.
Slowly drizzle in the oil through the feed tube, with the motor running. This quantity can very easily be doubled, so that you have plenty to use for other purposes. It keeps well in a covered jar in the refrigerator.

Fish Batter

1 cup flour
1 tsp baking powder
¼ tsp baking soda
½ tsp ground coriander (optional)
¼ tsp salt
1 cup water

Place the dry ingredients into a medium-sized bowl, then stir in the water with a spoon or fork until combined. This quantity is sufficient to coat 600-700g fish, cut into pieces or fingers, if the fillets you are using are thick. Pat the fish pieces dry with a paper towel before dipping them in the batter and deep frying in hot oil for about 2 minutes, more or less, depending on the size of the fish pieces.

This recipe is included under the same rationale as that outlined under Deep-Fried Mussels and Squid Rings on p.102 — it's simple and quick to make, economical and kids love it because it tastes just like fish 'n' chip shop batter.
You don't have to serve battered fish with chips — try baked or creamed potatoes instead — or allow the batter to serve as carbohydrate/energy and simply serve the battered fish with lemon wedges, steamed vegetables, and salads with fruit instead.

squid rings

Simple Poached Mussels

Poached mussels are superb as a simple entree, and need no embellishment. If you wish, you could reduce the liquid left after cooking the mussels to half by turning the heat up a little. Add 3 crushed garlic cloves and seasoning, then thicken with 1 tsp cornflour mixed with 2 tsp water to make a sauce which you can pour over the cooked mussels. This is optional, however, as poached mussels are juicy and succulent served straight from the pan, just as they are.

20-24 mussels, live in the shell
1½ cups water
1 tbsp lemon juice

Scrub the mussel shells and remove the beards by pulling gently.

Pour the water and lemon juice into a large shallow frypan or similar and heat to a simmer.

Add the mussels in their shells, cover and simmer gently for 3-5 minutes. The shells will open and the mussels will be tender and succulent.

Pile onto a heated serving plate to allow guests to help themselves. Prepare the sauce as outlined above if you wish, otherwise leave as they are.

Note: Instead of the water/lemon juice, you could use ¾ cup white wine/¾ cup water.

Specialty Smoked Seafoods

A very appealing range of smoked fish products is now available in vacuum packed, ready to eat form. Smoked mussels, smoked salmon and smoked eel are all sold in vacuum packs and although the last two are too expensive for everyday fare, a little of any of these tasty products can be spread a long way — and there's always the guarantee of a treat without a lot of preparation.

Usually they are served as appetisers, accompanied by crackers or slices of french bread or sushi (p.58), or as go anywhere lunches or suppers (from board room to beach) served with bagels, croissants or bread rolls and a selection of specialty cheeses such as joboe, natural smoked, gruyere or Swiss, fetta and blue vein, cucumber slices, tomato wedges, capsicum strips, lettuce, etc. plus some lemon juice to bring out the flavour or just a touch of mayonnaise.

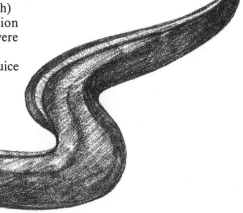

Smoked Eel Pâté

200g smoked eel
2½ tbsp lemon juice
1 tbsp lite sour cream (or sour cream)
freshly ground black pepper
1½ tsp capers

Place all the ingredients in a food processor and blend briefly, just to combine.
Cover and keep in the refrigerator until ready to serve.

Smoked eel is quite rich and has a definite flavour which is delicious in small quantities.

This recipe helps the eel go a little further, and by happy coincidence both mellows and enhances the flavour. Present with a strip or two of red capsicum and a sprig of dill or some other colourful garnish as the pâté is quite an insipid colour. The flavour, however, can well and truly stand on its own! Spread generously on fingers of fresh brown bread, this pâté is truly scrumptious.

Not recommended for freezing.

Nachos

I'm often asked for recipes for pre-dinner nibbles, dishes which are interesting, tasty, but not too filling. These nachos are easy to prepare but delicious, and they look quite stunning when presented attractively.

Salsa

2 tomatoes, skinned and roughly chopped
1 small capsicum, seeded and roughly chopped
2 tsp chilli sauce or sambal oelek (or to taste)
½ small onion
salt and freshly ground pepper to taste

Place all ingredients into a food processor and blend until smooth.
Now collect whatever quantity you need of:
— tortilla chips.
— sour cream.
— tasty grated cheddar cheese.
— slices of pimento-stuffed green olives.
Lay the chips in a single layer in a large, shallow, ovenproof dish.
Place some tasty grated cheddar on top of the chips.
Using two spoons, one to scoop off the other, place about ½ teaspoon of sour cream onto each tortilla chip.
Now place ½ teaspoon of the salsa onto the sour cream, followed by a slice of pimento-stuffed olive.
A few minutes before you want to serve the nachos, pre-heat your grill. Place the prepared nachos under the grill for just a few minutes, taking care not to burn them — just until the cheese melts. Wonderful!
Serve accompanied with serviettes and enjoy. You'll always need more than you think.

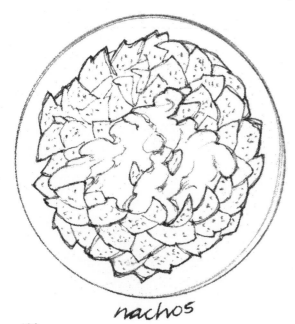

nachos

Tomato and Herb Dressing

¼ medium onion
2-3 cloves garlic, crushed
2 tbsp tomato paste
½ cup wine vinegar
¾ tsp salt
1 tbsp fresh chopped basil or oregano (try not to substitute 1 tsp dried)
1 tsp capers
½ tsp prepared mustard such as Dijon
1 cup oil

Place all the ingredients into the bowl of a food processor fitted with the metal blade.
Process for about 20 seconds, until well combined.
Pour into a lidded jar and keep in the refrigerator. Shake before serving over salads.

It's nice to have a change from vinaigrette dressing every now and then, without moving to a thicker or creamy mixture. This dressing is quite different and tastes great tossed with a green salad — so simple, too.

Blue Cheese Dressing

½ cup mayonnaise, preferably home-made (Place 1 egg, ½ tsp salt and 2 tbsp white or wine vinegar in a processor. Blend. Drizzle in 1 cup oil through feed tube while the motor is running. Makes 1 cup)
½ cup plain yoghurt
90g blue vein cheese, grated or crumbled
freshly ground black pepper

Place all the ingredients in a food processor and combine until smooth and creamy.

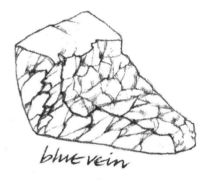
blue vein

This dressing has 'zing' without being too strong, and is a delightfully simple dressing for salads or dip for crudités such as raw celery and carrot sticks. It's also very nice on crackers or in sandwiches, combined with such things as tomato relish, cottage cheese and bean sprouts.

Sprouting Beans

Don't use horticultural seeds unless they are being sold for sprouting, as these may have been treated with chemicals for insect or fungus control.

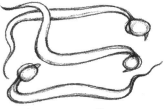

bean sprouts

In brief, any whole dried legume or seed may be sprouted. Sprouts not only taste good but they are valuable nutritionally; when a seed sprouts, its food value increases dramatically, especially in terms of its Vitamin C content, and some of the B group vitamins.

Favourite seeds to sprout are mung bean, brown lentil, alfalfa and chickpea. You could also try aduki beans and green soya beans (not the common dry variety, as they don't sprout so well). Mung beans and brown lentils take about the same time to sprout, so you can sprout them together if you wish.

It's a very simple and inexpensive matter to grow your own bean sprouts. Although there are a number of sprouting utensils on the market which are very good, all you really need is 1 or 2 glass 1-litre (preserving) jars with plastic screw-on lids which have had the centre removed and replaced by wire gauze. (These are available commercially in supermarkets and health food shops.)

Simply place about 1/3 cup of seeds into a jar, fill with cold water and leave for 8-12 hours or overnight. Drain off the water (or tip it into your favourite house plant, which will respond well) and rinse the seeds 3 times. Drain thoroughly, making sure that there is no excess water left in the bottom of the jar as this could cause the seeds to rot. Leave the jar sitting on your bench, but not in direct sunlight in the summer. Repeat this rinsing and draining twice a day until the sprouts are the size you want — usually about 3-5 days, depending on the warmth of the atmosphere and the type of sprout.

Keep the sprouts in a refrigerator. If for any reason they're unlikely to be used within 2-3 days, place them in a bowl of water in the refrigerator so that they remain crisp, changing the water every second day (up to 5 days).

All the above seeds are delicious sprouted and used liberally in salads, or on sandwiches in place of or with lettuce and other salad ingredients. (Our family special sandwich is peanut butter, home-made mayonnaise, sprouts, lettuce, beetroot and cheddar cheese.) They are also very nice in stir fries or omelettes, but they should not actually be cooked, just added at the last moment and heated through so that they retain their crisp texture and nutritional value.

Alfalfa seeds are probably the most popular of the sprouts, as they are especially delicate and ideal for salads or sandwiches. The same cannot really be said for chickpea sprouts, but these much larger and less attractive edibles are among my favourites. They taste quite like a fresh pea, lovely in salads/sandwiches, and a very valuable addition to stir fries or other cooked vegetable mixtures.

Cocktail Cheese Balls

250g cream cheese
2-3 spring onions, finely chopped
$^1/_4$ cup stuffed olives, chopped small and drained well (squeezed)
1-2 gherkins, finely chopped
1 clove garlic, crushed
$^1/_4$ cup flaked, toasted almonds
1 tbsp Thai sweet chilli sauce
freshly ground black pepper
toasted ground almonds, for coating

Soften the cream cheese slightly if needed.
Add the remaining ingredients and combine thoroughly.
Cover and place the mixture in the refrigerator to set for several hours.
Roll into marble-size balls, cover and refrigerate, preferably until just before serving.
Coat with the toasted ground almonds and present on a serving plate with crackers and a herb garnish.

Makes 50–60 small cheeseballs.

Trying to cut a slice of cheese off a wedge or spread cheese onto a cracker while balancing a glass of wine and a serviette can be quite a precarious exercise. The solution seems either to have specialty cheeses separated into individual slices and/or to produce these tasty individual cheese balls. Your guests can pick up a cheese ball, place it on a cracker and the exercise is completed quite neatly, with one hand and some style.
Best made the day before they are needed, they can be rolled and sit in the refrigerator until an hour or so before serving, when they can be rolled in toasted nuts and then either returned to the refrigerator or kept in a cool place until presented.

Fetta Dressing

This fresh-tasting dressing is delicious when served with a crisp vegetable and fruit salad. It looks creamy, but is in fact low in calories because of the proportion of plain yoghurt and fetta cheese it contains. Top a celery and apple salad with this, adding some nuts if you wish, or toasted pumpkin kernels. Or try dicing 2 unpeeled ripe pears, 2 stalks of celery and 1 zucchini. Add 1 cup sprouted beans (mung, alfalfa or chickpeas) and some finely chopped parsley.

Try a dollop on top of crisp steamed or microwaved shredded cabbage, too; you'll be surprised how a vegetable we take for granted can be transformed so simply!

½ cup plain yoghurt
½ cup grated fetta cheese
1 tbsp lemon juice
2 tsp runny or melted honey
½ cup mayonnaise (preferably home-made, p.102)
freshly ground black pepper

Place all the ingredients in a food processor or blender and blend until smooth and creamy.
Place in a jar with a screw-on lid, and keep in the refrigerator. It will keep for 4-5 days or more.

110

Nutty Spread

½ cup roasted peanuts
½ cup roasted sesame seeds
1 tsp oil
½ tsp salt
¼ cup water
1 tbsp olive oil
1 tsp soya sauce
¼ tsp sesame oil (optional)*

The easiest way to roast the peanuts and sesame seeds is to place them in a bowl with the 1 tsp oil and the salt and stir. Then microwave on high for 6 minutes, stirring after every 2 minutes or place the mixture in a pan and heat, stirring over a gentle heat until the nuts and seeds smell toasted and have turned a light golden colour.

Remove from the heat and allow to cool for 10 minutes or more.

Transfer the nut mixture to a food processor and process with the metal blade, until the ingredients are well ground (about 30 seconds).

With the motor running, pour in the water, olive oil, soya sauce and sesame oil if available. At this stage a spreadable paste will have formed which is delicious on fresh wholemeal bread, with or without other bits and pieces such as lettuce, hard-boiled eggs, mayonnaise, relish, etc.

Keep in a lidded jar in the pantry or refrigerator.

Nutty spread is nutritious, simply made and uses ingredients which are relatively inexpensive. The combination of legumes (peanuts) and seeds provides good quality protein, and it contains a much lower oil content than other nut spreads available commercially. Consequently it has a lighter texture and taste. You can enjoy a delicious nutty taste without consuming so much oil (fat).

Any vegetable oil could be used instead of sesame. Sesame does have a wonderful nutty flavour, however, so use it if you can.

Dill Pickles

Dill pickles take a little more time to prepare than sweet/sour gherkins, but many people prefer them because of their milder flavour. A few years ago I used to bottle over 100kg a year, some to give as gifts, but most to eat ourselves.

Children love them and they have a disturbing habit of simply disappearing whole out of the jar (empty jars have been found beneath beds and behind chairs in our house). These pickles are wonderful sliced into sandwiches, on biscuits with cheeses and served as part of an antipasto.

Dill is a most useful herb to have in your garden, as the leaves are used as flavouring for sauces and other savoury dishes. The immature (green) seeds are used as the flavouring in these pickles, and these should be picked before they dry. Use store-bought dried dill seeds only if you have to. Once you have dill in your garden, it will reappear year after year.

Ensure that the gherkins you use are firm and fresh. Size doesn't really matter, especially as the processed dills are usually sliced, although some people really prefer the 'Tom Thumb' size (10 cm or less). The middle-sized gherkins (10-15cm) are usually a little cheaper, however, and fit well into the litre jars. Scrub the gherkins if needed, and soak in cold water for at least 1 hour.

Pack them into clean 1-litre preserving jars — 15kg of gherkins will fill 25 litre jars approximately. Remember that the seal has to have space to sink down slightly in the middle, so cut a small piece off the end of any in danger of being in the way.

Now add to each litre jar:

1 sprig fresh dill seeds (about 20 seeds)
2 bay leaves
2 tsp salt
3 tsp sugar
1 tsp black peppercorns
½ tsp celery seed
1 tsp mustard seed
2 cloves garlic, peeled and slivered
1 dsp (12 ml) glacial acetic acid

Pour boiling water over the seals for the jars and leave to stand for 5 minutes. Fill each jar with hot water, almost to the top. Place on the seals and screw the ring bands on tightly.

Now place the filled jars into a water bath or a very large saucepan. If you do not have a water bath, you will probably need a saucepan especially for this purpose, unless you are using smaller jars. The bottom of this saucepan should be covered with crumpled foil or a rack, so that the jars do not sit on direct heat from the element. The jars should not touch each other. Fill the saucepan with hot water so that it just covers the top of the jars.

Cover and bring to the boil. Timing from that point, process for 10 minutes.

Remove the bottles from the water, preferably with a pair of tongs meant for the purpose, but don't tighten or loosen the ring bands. They can be removed when the bottles have cooled. If you can't see a definite dip in the seal after the bottles have cooled, the bottles have not sealed. These bottles may be kept in the refrigerator for 2-3 weeks and the pickles will be nice, though not as nice as those from sealed bottles.

Leave your pickles for as long as possible before opening — at least 2 weeks.

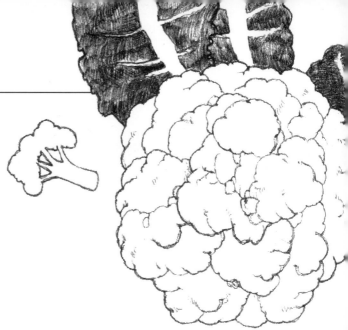

Turkish Mixed Pickles

Turkish Mixed Pickles are prepared in exactly the same way as the dill pickles. The dill may be omitted if you wish, although I recommend its inclusion, and/or 2-4 small dried chillies may be added to each jar if you wish.

It's best to make these pickles in the summer or autumn, when red capsicums are readily available, as these look so colourful in the jars. They're very attractive made with a simple mixture of cauliflower, zucchini and red capsicum, but choose any mixture you like from the list below. The vegetables must be fresh and firm and should be washed, but there is no need for soaking:

— cauliflorets, sliced lengthwise so that the slices are thin, but the shape of the floret is retained.

— red capsicum, seeded and sliced into small chunks.

— green capsicum, seeded and sliced into small chunks.

— small zucchini, sliced into 10 mm rounds.

— snow peas, sliced.

— beans, either butter or french, sliced into 5 cm pieces.

Pack the prepared vegetables into jars, then follow the procedure for dill pickles exactly.

These colourful pickles are a very pleasant accompaniment to many dishes, including cheeses and french bread, for a casual lunch.

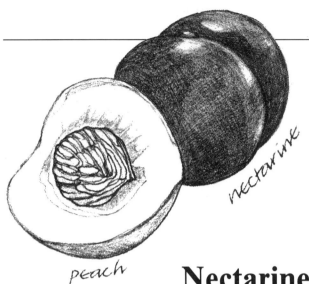

nectarine

peach

Nectarine or Peach Chutney

I feel as if I'm cheating a little with this recipe, since it is based on my mango chutney as published in *The Vegetarian Adventure Cook Book*. I was so pleased, however, to find that I could recreate it passably, and the procedure is a little different, so I think its publication here is justified.

This chutney has a wonderful flavour, and is ideal served as a sambal with curries, or as a condiment for cold meats. Try it, too, with cottage or other cheeses on savoury biscuits, sandwiches, etc.

*Golden Queen peaches may be substituted for the nectarines.

1 kg ripe but firm nectarines* (sometimes you can buy cheaper spotted ones which are still firm — just cut out the spots and weigh)
24 small red dried chillies (or more)
60g garlic, peeled
60g fresh root ginger, peeled and chopped roughly
4 cups brown sugar, packed
1¼ cups white sugar
600ml malt vinegar
40g mustard seeds

Weigh the nectarines.
Place the chillies, garlic and ginger in a food processor and chop until very fine. Place in a jam pan or large heavy-bottomed saucepan with the remaining ingredients except the nectarines and simmer until the syrup thickens, about 30 minutes.
Dice the unpeeled nectarines (stones and any bad pieces removed) and add to the syrup.
Simmer for approximately 1 more hour, stirring regularly.
Place a little of the chutney on a saucer and leave to cool for a few minutes. Nudge the top of the chutney with a fingertip; if the surface wrinkles, then the chutney is ready.
Pour into clean, hot sterilised jars and either cover with sealing wax and then cellophane covers or with screw-on lids which have had boiling water poured over them and have been left for 5 minutes.

Jan's Breakfast Hotcakes

1 cup rolled oats
1 cup milk (plus 2-3 tbsp extra if necessary)
2 tbsp brown sugar
2 eggs
2 tbsp fresh orange juice
½ cup oatbran
2 tsp baking powder
¼-½ tsp salt

Place the rolled oats in a bowl, pour in the milk and leave to stand while you grease a frypan and assemble the remaining ingredients.
Whisk the brown sugar, eggs and orange juice together with a fork, then add to the milk and oats. Add the oatbran, baking powder and the salt and combine with a spoon, gently but thoroughly. Add the extra milk if you feel the mixture is too thick — it should have a consistency similar to that of a thin pikelet batter.
Heat the greased frypan over a medium-high heat.
Place the batter in a jug for pouring, then pour in 2-3 tbsp of mixture, depending on whether you want pikelet- or pancake-sized hotcakes. Turn when bubbles appear and the underside is golden brown.
Serve as they come out of the pan, or stack 1-3 on individual plates.

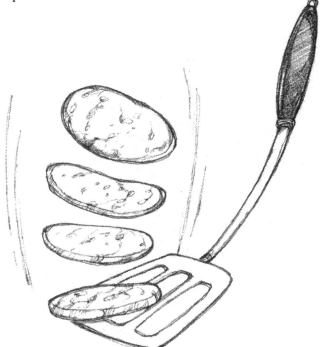

A friend of mine insisted that I try her American style hotcakes, a great favourite with her family. Suffice to say I had to make 2 batches on the morning I tried them. Here is the recipe, with a few small changes. My family decided they liked the addition of fresh orange juice in the actual mixture, although of course you can squeeze lemon or orange juice over the hotcakes once they have been mixed.
Oatbran is a nice addition to these hotcakes, which have a light wholemealy texture.
Try them with a light spread of runny bush honey, for example, then add topping variations such as sliced fresh kiwifruit, banana and coconut, passionfruit pulp, grated fresh apple, etc.

If you have children aged 12 or over (younger only with supervision), they can make hotcakes themselves in the weekends, leaving you in bed awaiting fresh hotcakes, served by a proud junior chef.

Hotcakes are also a highly nutritious and sustaining start to the day for youngsters whose Saturdays are filled with sports activities, especially in winter.

In the unlikely event that you have any left over, hotcakes can be frozen. Cool, then stack with a piece of freezer paper between each one. Place in freezer bags and tie securely. Allow to thaw, then reheat in a hot pan (or microwave).

115

Granola

Granola provides a really good start to the day, especially for growing children or adults who do a lot of exercise. For more sedentary adults it should be consumed in moderate amounts, however, especially if you have to watch your weight; as with all high energy foods, it is also quite high in calories.

Granola is the American name for muesli, and there are many variations on the basic theme. I feel that the packaged versions are quite expensive, but good value if you don't have a large family to feed. It is simple to make your own, however, and if stored in an airtight tin this quantity will keep well for weeks if necessary.

This recipe is my own version, but of course it's fun to experiment and find what suits your breakfast table best. Serve it with natural yoghurt, fresh fruit, milk, or whatever you feel like, whenever you like (my children often dip into it after school to eat it as a nibble).

Granola may be frozen, and although it may be microwaved, there seems little advantage when dealing with this quantity.

3 cups rolled oats
1 cup bran flakes
½ cup wheat germ
¼ cup sesame seeds
¾ cup chopped cashew nuts or pumpkin kernels
½ cup sunflower kernels
1 cup coconut
¼ cup peanut butter
½ cup oil
½ cup melted or runny honey
1 cup coarsely diced dried apricots
½ cup raisins

Pre-heat the oven to 150°C.
In a large bowl, mix together the first 7 ingredients.
In another bowl, mix together the peanut butter, oil and honey. Add these to the dry ingredients and mix well.
Spread the granola evenly into a medium-sized roasting pan or similar, then bake for 1-1¼ hours, stirring occasionally. Allow to cool for 10 minutes, then add the dried fruit and mix well.
When completely cool, place in an airtight tin and store.

apricots + raisins

Desserts and Fillings For Those Gaps

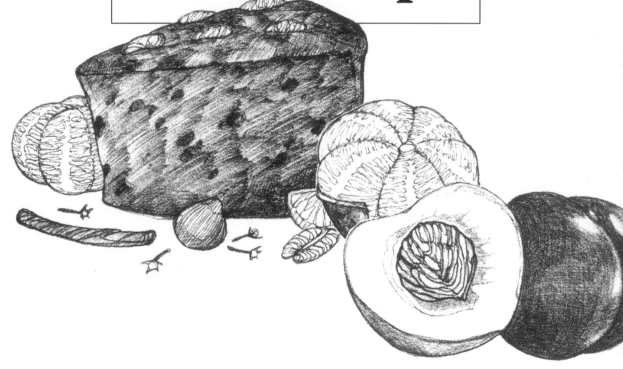

Blueberry and Spice Ice Cream

Ice cream is everybody's favourite, although it really is quite difficult to achieve a better product than is available in New Zealand commercially. This blueberry ice cream, though, with its subtle hint of orange and spice, seems to find favour with everybody, especially when drizzled with blueberry sauce and served with fresh seasonal fruits.

A processor is used for this ice cream. Although it is possible to make it with an electric or hand beater, a processor doesn't aerate the mixture as much, so allowing excess water crystals to form and the ice cream to 'ice'. The blueberries are not strained in this recipe, because the texture is quite appealing. Strain the cooked berries if you prefer, though.

Ensure that your egg whites are at room temperature, and that the whipping cream is chilled.

2 cups blueberries, fresh or frozen (300g)
2 tbsp sugar
¼ cup orange juice
1 tsp grated orange zest
½ tsp whole grated nutmeg, preferably, or ¾ tsp ground
4 egg whites
½ cup sugar
300ml whipping cream
2 tbsp slivered almonds (optional)

Place the blueberries, first measure of sugar, the orange juice and the zest in a saucepan or suitable jug, for microwaving. Bring to the boil over a gentle heat, stirring occasionally, then simmer until the berries are tender and split — about 8 minutes (or microwave). Cool completely — refrigerate if possible — until ready to add to the rest of the mixture.

Separate the eggs and place the whites in a food processor bowl with the whipping blade. (Reserve the yolks for use in mayonnaise or sauces if you wish.) Beat the whites until they 'peak'. Add the second measure of sugar gradually while the motor is running, until a thick, shiny meringue forms. Transfer the meringue mixture to a bowl.

Pour the cream into the processor bowl and beat until it holds a soft peak. Pour the whipped cream into the meringue mixture and combine gently but thoroughly.

Now fold in ½ cup of the blueberry mixture, just until it is partially combined. Swirls of this sauce in the ice cream give a pleasing taste and visual effect.

Pour the ice cream carefully into a plastic container with a lid, or cover with cling wrap and freeze for 8-12 hours, until firm.

Serve drizzled with reserved blueberry sauce — you should have about ½ cup left, sufficient to drizzle over 6 servings of ice cream.

Summer Pudding

**750g total weight of frozen berries such as a combination of
raspberries, blueberries, boysenberries, redcurrants, etc.**
175ml water
225g sugar
juice of ½ lemon
1 tbsp gelatine, softened in ¼ cup water or juice from thawing berries
**thinly sliced white bread, preferably from a day old uncut loaf, or
  sliced bread left out of the packet to dry (crusts off).**

Allow the berries to thaw overnight or partially defrost them so
that you can soak the gelatine in ¼ cup of the resulting liquid.
Place all the fruit and any remaining juices into a bowl and mash
lightly.
Bring the water and sugar to the boil, simmer for 1–2 minutes,
then remove from the heat and add lemon juice and the softened
gelatine.
Stir until the gelatine is dissolved.
Pour the syrup over the fruit and mix.
Line a bowl with Gladwrap and line with crustless slices of bread.
You will have to cut these to fit neatly, trying not to leave any gaps.
Scoop the fruit and syrup into the bread-lined bowl.
Arrange slices of bread to make a neat fit over the top.
Fold the excess Gladwrap over this and place a side plate or
similar to create a lid on which you can position cans of fruit or
some such to weight the pudding down lightly.
Leave it at room temperature for an hour so that the syrup will
soak into the bread before the gelatine sets.
Store in the refrigerator for at least a day and up to 3 before
serving.

The fresh berry flavours and
rich red colour of this dessert
make it especially welcome,
ironically, at the end of winter
— when thoughts are *turning*
to summer. This recipe uses
frozen berries instead of fresh,
so that it not only can be
served out of season — but
even better, it can be made 3
days ahead.
Sometimes I serve it with a
raspberry coulis (also made
with frozen berries) and at
other times simply with lightly
whipped cream and a garnish.

Strawberries

Strawberries are so delicious in their sweet, natural state, that there's little incentive to do too much to them. One hint, though, for something a little different, is to hull and slice the fresh berries into a bowl, sprinkle over a little sugar to your taste, followed by a dash of blackberry nip! Sounds so simple, but the flavour is enhanced by this treatment, and if you are having guests for dinner, what could be simpler, served with a special ice cream, perhaps, or fresh whipped cream.

Blueberry and Apple Crumble

This easy dessert will appeal to all crumble topping lovers — baked apples and blueberries with lots of crunchy, spice-laced topping.

This recipe may be microwaved, for 12-15 minutes on full power using a 20-23cm diameter dish. Fine timing is dependent on whether the blueberries are frozen or fresh, and on what size dish you are using, (Microwave the larger dish for the shorter time.)

3-4 medium apples, such as Granny Smiths
1½ cups blueberries, fresh or frozen

Grate the unpeeled apples into a shallow dish about 30 x 20cm.
Cover with the blueberries.

Crumble Topping
¾ cup brown sugar
½ cup flour
1½ cup rolled oats
1 tsp cinnamon
100g butter or margarine, chopped into 6 pieces

Pre-heat the oven to 190°C.
Place all the crumble ingredients into a food processor bowl, adding the butter last, and process briefly or rub the butter into the dry ingredients with your fingers.
Sprinkle the crumble topping evenly over the top of the fruit (this is quite a substantial topping) and bake for 40-45 minutes.
Eat hot or at room temperature, with or without ice cream, custard, cream or milk.

Topsy Apple Cake

100g margarine or butter
¾ cup brown sugar (first measure)
1 tsp cinnamon
¼ cup ground almonds
2 smallish apples such as Granny Smiths
½ cup sultanas
2 eggs
1 cup brown sugar (second measure)
½ cup plain yoghurt
½ cup wholemeal flour
1 cup plain flour
1 tsp baking soda
1 tsp baking powder
¾ tsp ground nutmeg
½ tsp ground allspice
½ cup cottage cheese

Topsy Apple Cake is delicious and very suitable for colder weather. It's a great family favourite, accompanied by custard if you wish, and some whipped cream or ice cream.

Pre-heat the oven to 180°C.
Butter a 20cm ring tin.
Beat the softened margarine or butter and the first measure of brown sugar together with a wooden spoon, then spread evenly over the bottom of the ring tin.
Sprinkle the ground almonds evenly over the top of the margarine/sugar mixture, then cover with the grated, unpeeled apples.
Now sprinkle the sultanas over the apples.
Place the eggs and the second measure of brown sugar in a food processor and cream together.
Add the yoghurt, then the flours, baking soda, baking powder, nutmeg, allspice and cottage cheese.
Process for about 30 seconds, just until well combined, then pour evenly into the ring tin on top of the other ingredients.
Bake at 180°C for 30-40 minutes or until a skewer inserted into the cake comes out clean.
Tip onto a serving plate and cut into wedge slices.
Accompany with custard and whipped cream or ice cream if serving for dessert.
Any leftovers may be frozen; this makes quite a large dessert.

>and cinnamon?

121

Apples en Croute

This dish is simple and quick to make. It can be prepared ahead and left in the refrigerator until you're ready to cook, it looks impressive and it tastes great. All these criteria are important when you have little time to spare, so it really is a worthwhile dish to become familiar with.

Filo (phyllo) pastry comes sealed inside a plastic 'sleeve' inside the packet. It's worthwhile slipping this out to have a quick look at the pastry before you buy. Fresh pastry shouldn't appear flaky or dry — if it does, it may have been stored inadequately, or it could have been kept for too long.

²/₃ **cup currants or mixture of currants and chopped raisins**
4 tbsp roughly chopped walnuts
½ cup brown sugar
4 tbsp orange juice (or rum)
2 tsp ground cinnamon
½ tsp ground cloves
6 smallish cooking apples, preferably Granny Smiths
6 sheets filo (phyllo) pastry
100g butter, approx., melted
¼ cup dry breadcrumbs
6-10 whole cloves

Mix the dried fruits, walnuts, brown sugar, orange juice and spices together in a small bowl to allow the flavours to blend while you prepare the other ingredients.
Peel the apples and core them. Melt the butter.
Stuff the apples firmly with the dried fruit/spice mixture.
Take 1 sheet of filo pastry and place it so that the long side is in front of you. Brush this with melted butter, then place another sheet on top of the first. Brush this top sheet with melted butter also, then sprinkle lightly with ¹/₃ of the dry breadcrumbs.
Pre-heat the oven to 190°C.
Cut the sheet into 2 halves, then place a stuffed apple in the middle of each half. Bring 1 edge of the pastry up over the top of the first apple and continue wrapping the apple in the pastry until you have a neat round 'parcel'. Pleat the pastry in layers at the top of the apple as you go, then secure this with a whole clove when you have completed the parcel.
Now brush the whole pastry parcel with melted butter and place on a greased oven dish. Repeat this entire process with the other 5 apples.
The prepared apples may be refrigerated at this stage until you are ready to bake them.
Bake at 190°C for 30-35 minutes.
Spoon some of the sauce which will have escaped to the bottom of the dish over the top of the apples, to give them a 'glaze', and serve individually with fresh whipped cream or ice cream.
Note: These apples can be frozen if slightly undercooked. Reheat in a pre-heated oven from frozen, and ensure that they are hot right through before serving.

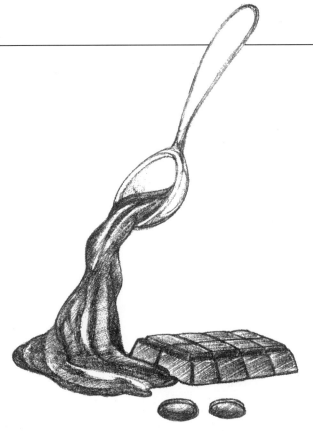

Super Quick Chocolate Sauce

3 tbsp cocoa
¹/₃ cup icing sugar
6 tbsp margarine (90g)

Place the above ingredients in a bowl or small saucepan. Microwave on medium power for 1 minute, stirring to combine after 40 seconds or melt together over a very gentle heat or in a double boiler.
Whisk smooth, then serve immediately over ice cream.

This sauce doesn't strictly come into the category of 'health' food, of course, but a case could be argued that a long-term plan for healthy living involves balance, moderation, common sense *and* variety in what you eat. It's a rare person, after all, who never allows themselves any dietary indulgences. The main advantage of this sauce is the speed with which it can be prepared. All you need is some ice cream, and some fresh fruit as well, preferably.
It's a great standby when unexpected guests arrive and there's never any shortage of helpers if there are children in the house. If allowed to sit on top of the ice cream for a minute or two the sauce sets, rather like a chocolate dip. (Hence the relatively high proportion of margarine — but you only need a small amount to top each serve.) Serve the fresh fruit as a fruit salad, or sliced on a central platter for individuals to serve themselves.

Not recommended for freezing.

Kiwifruit and Citrus Flan

The flavours of oranges and lemons combine perfectly with fresh kiwifruit to create this flan. Try it as a stunning conclusion to a dinner for friends. It looks wonderful, tastes superb, but is simple and economical to make.

*It's a simple matter to make your own caster sugar by placing ordinary granulated sugar in a food processor. Process using the steel blade for 1 minute.

Pastry
1½ cups plain flour
⅓ cup caster sugar*
100g cold butter, cut into 8 pieces
1 egg
1-2 tbsp iced water

Filling
1 egg
⅓ cup sugar
2 tsp finely grated orange zest
2 tbsp fresh orange juice
1 tsp finely grated lemon zest
2 tbsp fresh lemon juice
2 tbsp sour cream or whipping cream

Topping
5-6 kiwifruit, peeled, depending on size
1-2 tbsp honey or apricot jam for glaze

Process the flour, caster sugar and butter in a food processor using the steel blade until the mixture resembles breadcrumbs.

With the motor running, add the egg, followed quickly by enough of the cold water for the mixture to begin to 'ball'.

Wrap the dough in plastic wrap and place in the refrigerator for at least 30 minutes, preferably more — this is quite a soft dough and longer refrigeration means easier handling.

Pre-heat the oven to 200°C.

Roll out the dough to fit a greased 23cm flan dish, preferably with a removable base. You may have a little dough left over, but the pastry should not be too thin as you don't want the filling to leak through.

Place some aluminium foil over the lined dish, making sure to cover the sides as well. Cover the bottom with dried beans or rice. (Keep some for just this purpose, and re-use it.)

Bake the flan shell at 200°C for 20 minutes, then remove the rice or beans and the foil. Allow to cool.

Reduce the oven heat to 160°C.

Place all the filling ingredients into a food processor and process for approximately 20 seconds.

Pour the citrus filling into the cooled shell, then bake at the reduced oven heat for about 15 minutes, until the filling is set.

Allow to cool to room temperature, removing the sides of your flan tin if you are using a springform tin.

When the flan is cool, peel the kiwifruit and slice thinly. Arrange the slices over the top of the flan so that they overlap in a circular pattern.

Heat or microwave the honey or apricot jam until it begins to boil, then brush this over the kiwifruit slices, taking care not to press too firmly.

Serve the flan at room temperature, accompanied by whipped cream if you wish.

Spiced Oatbran Scones

These scones are light and spicy, and take only a few minutes to make.

Not recommended for microwaving; freezes well.

1½ cups plain flour
1 cup oatbran (or wholemeal flour)
4 tsp baking powder
1 tsp baking soda
1 tsp ground ginger
1 tsp ground allspice
1 tsp cinnamon
50g butter or margarine
1/3 cup brown sugar (packed)
½-¾ cup sultanas
¾ cup milk
¼ cup warm water

Pre-heat the oven to 220°C.
Place the flour, oatbran, baking powder and spices in a bowl and mix well.
Rub or cut in the butter or margarine, then add the sugar and the sultanas and combine.
Make a well in the centre then pour in the milk and the warm water, mixing to a soft dough with a knife.
Turn the dough out onto a lightly floured board, knead it 3-4 times, then pat it into a circle shape, about 2.5cm thick.
Cut the round into tenths or twelfths, using a sharp knife, and place on an ungreased baking tray.
Bake at 220°C for about 12 minutes.

Blueberry Pinwheels

1½ cups plain flour
½ cup wholemeal flour
4 tsp baking powder
50g margarine or butter
¾-1 cup plain yoghurt or milk
¼ cup coconut
¼ cup brown sugar, packed (generous)
1 tsp cinnamon
¹/₃ cup frozen or fresh blueberries

Pre-heat the oven to 200°C.
Place the flours and baking powder into a bowl and cut or rub in the margarine or butter.
Make a well in the centre, and pour in ¾ cup yoghurt or milk then mix in with a knife. The mixture should start to 'ball' away from the sides of the bowl without overmixing. If not, add a little more of the milk or yoghurt, up to 1 cup in total.
Turn out onto a lightly floured board and knead lightly, about 6 times. Now pat or roll out to make a 30cm square approximately.
Mix the coconut, brown sugar and cinnamon together, and sprinkle evenly over the top of the dough. Press very lightly with the back of a spoon or the palms of your hands so that the sugar mixture compacts slightly and will stay where it's meant to. Now sprinkle over the frozen or fresh blueberries and roll up tightly. Flour the blade of a sharp knife and cut into 2.5cm slices.
Lay the pinwheels on their sides on an oven slide.
Bake at 200°C for 15-20 minutes.

It's lovely to have a bag or two of frozen blueberries in the freezer. They free-flow freeze so well and can be used just as you use fresh berries, to make scones such as these, muffins or cakes, all at a moment's notice. These pinwheels are very popular, and just a bit different from ordinary scones. Serve them with lunches, with morning coffee or to take on picnics.

Yoghurt makes these scones extra light and gives an appearance which is a bit more 'puffy' than those mixed with milk.

May be microwaved, but bake for preference. They freeze well.

Citrus Poppyseed Cake

This superb recipe comes from the Vine Cafe in the Isles of Scilly. Light, simple, redolent of citrus and sun, this cake is ideal to present at the end of a special lunch with friends, or as a very different dessert cake served with a spoonful of cream.

* The amount of poppy seeds used does seem a little excessive — but without this quantity the cake would lose some of its unique texture and character.

250g margarine or softened butter
250g sugar
4 eggs, separated
250g sour cream
grated rind of 2 oranges and 4 lemons
250g plain flour
1 tsp baking powder
1 tsp baking soda
190g poppy seeds*

Cream the margarine and sugar until light and fluffy.
Add the egg yolks, sour cream and fruit rinds.
Sift in the flour, baking powder and baking soda.
Whisk the egg whites until stiff but not dry.
Fold in the egg whites, followed by the poppy seeds.
Pour the batter into a 20cm square tin lined with baking paper.
Bake at 190° C for approximately 1 hour, or until a skewer inserted into the cake comes out clean,
Turn out onto a tray or plate with a lip and prick all over.
While the cake is baking, juice the 2 oranges and 4 lemons and place the juices in a saucepan with 250g sugar. Bring to the boil, then remove from the heat and drizzle all over the still hot cake (both the cake and the sauce should be hot), easing the cake up with a knife so the juices soak the underneath of the cake as well. All the juice should be used.
This cake may be frozen, and keeps well in the refrigerator for several days.

Kiwifruit or Apple Oatbran Muffins

1 cup kiwifruit chopped small (about 4 medium kiwifruit) or 1-1½ apples
1 cup plain flour
1 cup oatbran (or wholemeal flour)
½ cup sugar
2 tsp baking powder
2 tsp ground nutmeg
50g margarine, melted
½ cup milk
½ tsp white vinegar or lemon juice
1 egg, lightly beaten

Pre-heat the oven to 220°C.
Peel the kiwifruit and dice the flesh small or grate the unpeeled apple(s). You should have about 1 cup of kiwifruit flesh or grated apple.
Mix the flour, oatbran, sugar, baking powder and nutmeg in a bowl.
Melt the margarine and sour the milk with the white vinegar.
Mix the margarine, soured milk and lightly beaten egg together, then pour into the dry ingredients and combine thoroughly.
Add the prepared kiwifruit and combine again.
Grease 12 large muffin tins and spoon the mixture evenly into these.
Bake at 220°C for 12-15 minutes.
Allow to sit in the tins for a few minutes, then remove and cool on a cake rack.

In these days of cholesterol awareness oatbran has achieved a pinnacle of recognition among seekers of soluble fibre to help reduce blood cholesterol levels. For us prevention-is-better-than-cure advocates, too, it is wise to include some oatbran in your diet as and when you can. There are, however, many sources of soluble fibre in the plant world though they may not be so concentrated as in oatbran; unless you have a medical condition, it shouldn't be regarded as a panacea in itself. Include it where you can, and keep in mind that the key to a healthy diet you can live with is moderation, balance, common sense and lots of variety.
The fact that these muffins contain oatbran is one thing; the fact that they taste positively scrumptious is another.

These muffins may be microwaved (half-fill muffin cups, then microwave on high for 3 minutes) but for appearance and texture I recommend oven baking. Freezes well.

You could try this recipe using other fruits, such as feijoas.

129

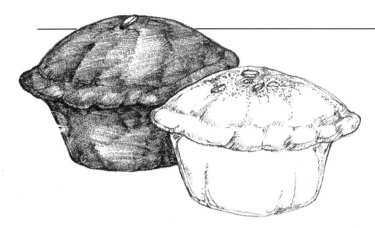

Avocado, Lemon and Herb Muffins

Avocados are so delicious served simply sprinkled with lemon juice and a smidgen of seasoning that it seems a shame to eat them in any other form. These savoury muffins, though, have a unique flavour and texture — lovely for a change when avocados are plentiful. Serve them for breakfast, lunch or with a soup for dinner.

Muffins are always best eaten soon after they are made, but if this isn't possible, they freeze well. Not recommended for microwaving.

Don't expect the avocado flavour to be overpowering in these muffins; it is discernible, though, and combines very well with the lemon/herb/cheese flavours. These muffins are high in fibre content and also contain a good proportion of protein. One average-sized avocado contains nearly as much protein as a 500g T-bone steak, and only a quarter of the fat.

1 cup plain flour
1 cup oatbran (or wholemeal flour)
2 tsp baking powder
1 tsp baking soda
½ tsp salt
1 tsp finely chopped fresh oregano or ⅓ tsp dried
3 tbsp finely chopped chives or 2 tbsp grated onion
1-2 tbsp finely chopped parsley
½ cup grated tasty cheddar cheese (packed)
50g margarine or butter
1 tsp grated lemon rind (zest)
1 tbsp lemon juice
1 egg
¾ cup milk
⅓ cup ripe avocado flesh, diced small (about ½ small avocado)

Pre-heat oven to 200°C.
Place the flour, oatbran, baking powder, baking soda and salt in a bowl and combine. Add the oregano, chives, parsley and cheese and mix again.
Melt the margarine or butter. Add the lemon rind and juice to the melted margarine and whisk in the egg with a fork, then add the milk.
Make a well in the dry ingredients, pour in the egg/milk mixture and stir. Lastly, add the diced avocado flesh and fold in — there should be no flour 'pockets' lurking at the bottom of the bowl, but don't overmix.
Grease large muffins tins and fill almost to the top with the mixture.
Bake at 200°C for 12-15 minutes. Allow the muffins to sit in their tins for a few minutes before turning out onto a cake rack.
This recipe makes 12 large muffins.

Energy Loaf

1 cup wholemeal flour
½ cup sugar
1 cup bran flakes
1 cup sultanas
1 cup milk
2 tbsp golden syrup
1 tsp baking soda

This beautifully moist and fruity loaf is ideal for school lunches or after-school appetites. It's also very quick and simple to make.

Pre-heat the oven to 180°C.
Grease and line the bottom of a loaf tin with greaseproof paper.
Place the flour, sugar and the bran flakes in a bowl and mix well.
Heat the milk and the golden syrup together in a saucepan (or microwave). Remove from the heat and add the baking soda. Quickly pour the heated ingredients into the bowl with the flour, sugar and bran. Combine well.
Bake at 180°C for 30-40 minutes.
Turn out onto a cake rack to cool, and remove the lining paper.

Coconut Loaf

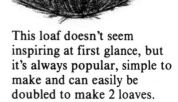

1 heaped cup of plain flour
1 tsp baking powder
½ tsp salt
¾ cup sugar
1 cup desiccated coconut
¾-1 cup milk

Place all the dry ingredients into a bowl and mix well.
Add the milk and combine.
Bake in a greased and lined loaf tin for 40-50 minutes at 180°C.
Turn out and cool on rack.

This loaf doesn't seem inspiring at first glance, but it's always popular, simple to make and can easily be doubled to make 2 loaves.

Gingerbread

This is another old favourite, easy to make and great for families. A good one for young cooks, too — let them do the cooking for a change and you'll all enjoy the results.

250g butter
2 cups sugar
½ cup golden syrup
2 tsp baking soda
2 cups milk
4 tsp ginger
2 tsp cinnamon
2 tsp cocoa
4 cups flour

Pre-heat the oven to 180°C.
Melt the butter, sugar and golden syrup in a saucepan over a low heat.
Stir the baking soda into the milk, then add this to the mixture.
Add the sifted ginger, cinnamon, cocoa and flour and mix well, preferably using a hand whisk or small electric beater to combine all the ingredients.
Grease and line the bottoms of 2 loaf tins with greaseproof paper. Pour in the mixture, dividing it equally between the 2 tins. Push the mixture into the corners of the tins with a spatula and smooth the top of each loaf.
Bake at 180°C for about 45 minutes, then test with a skewer. If it comes out clean, the gingerbread is ready.
Turn out onto a cake rack and remove the lining paper.
Slice and spread thinly with butter when cool, or serve with custard as a dessert.

Pumpkin Cake

2 eggs
½ cup oil
1 heaped cup sugar
1 cup cooked mashed pumpkin
1²/₃ cups plain flour
½ tsp each of ground cloves, cinnamon, nutmeg and ginger
¼ tsp baking soda
1 tsp baking powder

Turn the oven to 180°C.
Place the eggs, oil and sugar in a large bowl. Beat well (an electric beater is best) until they are thick and creamy.
Add the pumpkin and mix until well combined.
Sift the remaining ingredients and add to the bowl. Fold in carefully.
Grease a loaf tin, then line the bottom of it with butter paper. Pour the mixture into the prepared tin, pushing it well into the corners and evening out the top.
Bake at 180°C for 1 hour. Test if it is cooked by pushing a skewer into the middle. If it comes out clean, the cake is cooked.
Leave it to sit for 5 minutes, then remove from the tin. Peel off the bottom lining paper and cool on a cake rack.

This pumpkin cake is very simple to make, but scrumptious just the same. If you have children aged between 8 and 12, you could suggest they try making this loaf/cake, with a bit of supervision for the younger group. Once they've got the idea it certainly saves wear and tear on parents!

Not recommended for microwaving; freezes well.

Muesli Biscuits

1 cup rolled oats
1 cup wholemeal flour
¾ cup sugar
1 cup coconut
1 cup sultanas or ¾ cup chopped, pitted dates plus ¼ cup chopped dried apricots
180g margarine or butter, melted
3 tbsp golden syrup (or honey)
1 tsp baking soda dissolved in 2 tbsp hot water

Place the dry ingredients in a bowl and mix well together. Mix the melted margarine and syrup with the baking soda and hot water, and quickly pour into the dry ingredients. Mix well.
Place in tablespoon lots on a greased baking tray, flattening them a little.
Bake until golden brown at 180°C for about 10-15 minutes, taking care that they don't burn.

muesli cookies

These biscuits are not only extremely easy and quick to make, but they taste wonderful. Crisp and chewy, they are favourites of both children and adults. The only problem is that they are gone almost as soon as you make them.

Gingered Pumpkin and Pineapple Pie

This very popular pie was conceived in response to frustration at never finding a pumpkin pie recipe I really loved. Although I can't legitimately call this creation a pumpkin pie, I feel that the end result has justified taking a few liberties.

Base

1 cup crushed gingernuts OR
¹/₂ cup crushed gingernuts and ¹/₂ cup crushed wine biscuits
75g melted butter

Line the bottom of a 20 cm cake tin (with a lift out base) with baking paper and press the biscuit mixture in firmly.
Bake at 180° C for 8–10 minutes then remove from the oven and allow to cool.

Filling

2 eggs
1 cup brown sugar
³/₄ cup cooked, mashed pumpkin
1 tsp cornflour
1 440g tin crushed, very well drained pineapple (squeeze out)
¹/₂ cup coconut cream

Beat the eggs and the sugar until thick.
Fold in the remaining ingredients.
Pour into the cooled base, then bake at 180° C for 50–55 minutes, until the filling is evenly firm to the touch.
Allow to cool for at least 10 minutes before removing from the tin.

Rhubarb Tart/Fruit Slice

Base and Topping

¹/₂ cup walnuts
1 cup rolled oats
1 cup plain flour
¹/₂ cup dessicated coconut
¹/₂ cup bran
1 cup brown sugar
2 tsp ground ginger
1 tsp baking powder
175g cold butter, chopped

Place all the ingredients for the base and topping into a food processor in the order given, and process until well combined.
Press half of the mixture into a Swiss roll tin or similar.
Spread the rhubarb or other fruit filling evenly over this, then sprinkle the remaining mixture over the top.
Bake for approximately 25 minutes at 190° C. Cut into bar shapes when cool.

Filling

350g trimmed raw rhubarb (or raw or frozen fruit of your choice)*
¹/₃ cup sugar
1¹/₂ tbsp custard powder

Chop the trimmed rhubarb into 5–8 cm lengths and place in processor bowl with the sugar and process until chopped small and combined. Add the custard powder and pulse until combined.

Rhubarb is a very useful plant to have growing at the back of your garden. It needs very little tending, and just keeps on growing year after year. My children enjoy eating the stems raw, but it is more commonly enjoyed cooked and sweetened.

I have noted a resurgence of interest in tart fruit flavours, and they are certainly a favourite of mine. Raspberries, red currants, gooseberries, tamarillos or plums could all be used for this slice.

* Frozen or tinned fruit can also be used, though you should drain any excess liquid from tinned fruit if using and decrease the sugar content to 4–5 tbsp unless they are unsweetened.

This square, with its oaty shortcake base and topping, is popular with both children and adults. It's delicious to serve with coffee, or as a dessert accompanied by whipped cream, plain yoghurt or icecream. (Best served the day it is made.)

rhubarb

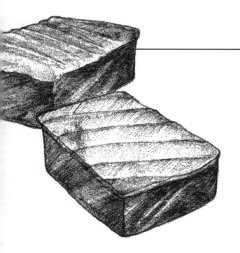

Fudge Square

125g butter
½ cup sugar
1 tbsp cocoa
1 tbsp golden syrup
1 cup flour
½ cup desiccated coconut or rolled oats
1 tsp baking powder
chocolate icing (optional)

This simple square is a great favourite and so simple that children over 8 can make it themselves (the assumption being that they'll be the main consumers of it — adults, of course, will be much too self-restrained). Above all, it's quick to make and can easily be doubled.

This square is very nice uniced — and it seems to disappear just as quickly.

Pre-heat the oven to 180°C.
Place the butter, sugar, cocoa and golden syrup in a saucepan or bowl for microwaving. Melt, stirring occasionally, but don't boil.
Remove the saucepan from the heat, then add the flour, the coconut and the baking powder. Mix well.
Press the mixture into a greased sponge roll tin.
Bake at 180°C for exactly 10 minutes.
When the square is cool, ice it with chocolate icing if you wish and cut it into squares. Keep it either in an airtight tin or in the refrigerator.

Peanut Brownies

Peanut Brownies are something I remember with affection from childhood. I had great difficulty, however, in trying to faithfully reproduce the light, crisp, nutty morsels I remember. Persistence won out, and these biscuits have now been a family favourite for many years.

This recipe may be doubled.

125g margarine or butter
1 scant cup sugar
1 egg
1 cup flour
½ tsp baking powder
3 tbsp cocoa
1½ cups raw peanuts

Cream the butter and sugar in a food processor. Add the egg and beat well. Add the flour, baking powder and cocoa and process to combine. Transfer the mixture to a bowl and mix in the peanuts with a spoon.
Place the mixture in heaped teaspoon lots on a greased oven tray and bake at 180°C for approximately 15 minutes.
Remove and cool on a cake rack.

Mandarin Spiced Fruit Cake

1 312g tin of mandarin segments in light syrup, drained
¼ cup reserved mandarin syrup
600g dried mixed fruit
1 tsp ground cinnamon
½ tsp ground nutmeg
1 tsp ground cloves
1 tsp ground ginger
125g margarine or butter
½ cup brown sugar
3 eggs
1½ cups plain flour
½ cup wholemeal flour
2 tsp baking powder
1 cup milk
½ cup walnut or pecan pieces, or roughly chopped
extra walnut or pecan halves (optional)

Drain the mandarin segments, reserving ¼ cup of the syrup. Chop the mandarin segments small — you should have about ½ cup mandarin flesh.

Place the mixed dried fruit into a large bowl, then add the mandarin segments, the reserved ¼ cup of syrup and the spices to the fruit. Mix well, then set aside. This is best left for at least 30 minutes.

Pre-heat the oven to 160°C and line the base of a greased 20cm ring tin with greaseproof paper.

Cream the margarine and sugar together, then add the eggs one by one, beating well after each addition. You can use a food processor for this step.

Add the creamed mixture with the flour, baking powder, milk and walnut pieces to the dried fruit and mandarin mixture. Fold in gently but thoroughly to combine.

Pour the mixture evenly into the prepared ring tin and decorate the top with the extra walnut or pecan halves if you wish. Bake for approximately 1½ hours at 160°C, or until a skewer inserted into the middle of the mixture comes out clean.

Leave to stand in the tin for 10 minutes, then invert onto a cake rack, remove the lining paper and allow to cool. Best not cut for at least 12 hours.

This cake is a favourite, a delightful blend of mandarin and fruit richly laced with spice which has proved very popular with everyone who has tried it.

It makes an ideal Christmas cake for people who prefer a lighter, but special and unusual cake instead of a very traditional one. It's also very useful to have as a pre-Christmas cake, when people call to 'catch up' before the New Year rolls round, but it's not prohibitively expensive to make, so it can be made and produced as a 'special' fruitcake at any time of the year.

It is possible to make this cake with ½ plain, ½ wholemeal flour; and/or delete the walnuts. The results are still excellent, but the measures given here are my pick for the best combination of flavour, texture and appearance.

Fruitcakes keep best in a cool place if you're not going to eat them quickly. Freezes well. Not recommended for microwaving.

Index

bay leaves

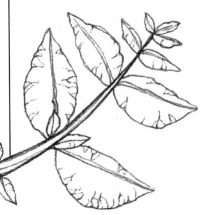

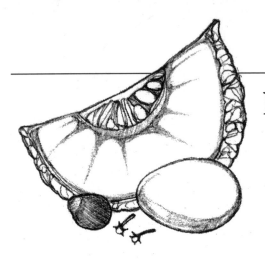

Notes